Frommer's®

SO-BLD-761

100

Best Beaches
1st Edition

by Holly Hughes

WILEY

John Wiley & Sons, Inc.

Contents

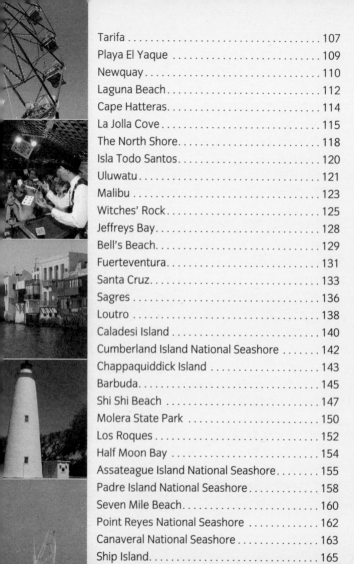

Published by:

John Wiley & Sons, Inc.

111 River St.
Hoboken, NJ 07030-5774

ISBN 978-1-118-16493-8

Editor: Cate Latting
Production Editor: M. Faunette Johnston
Photo Editors: Cherie Cincilla, Alden Gewirtz & John Vorwald
Interior book design: Melissa Auciello-Brogan
Production by Wiley Indianapolis Composition Services

Front cover photo: Spectacular sunrise looking south from Ecola State Park over Crescent Beach toward Cannon Beach, Oregon © Peter Haigh/Alamy Images. Back cover photo: Captiva and Sanibel Island, Florida © Chad McDermott/ Alamy Images.

For information on our other products and services or to obtain technical support, please contact our Customer Care Department within the U.S. at 877/ 762-2974, outside the U.S. at 317/572-3993 or fax 317/572-4002.

Wiley also publishes its books in a variety of electronic formats. Some content that appears in print may not be available in electronic formats.

Manufactured in the United States of America

5 4 3 2 1

About the Author

Holly Hughes has traveled the globe as a writer and editor. A former executive editor of Fodor's Guides, she now edits the popular annual *Best Food Writing* anthologies, as well as co-authoring a number of Frommer's titles – most recently *Frommer's 500 Places to Take Your Kids Before They Grow Up*, *Frommer's 500 Places to See Before They Disappear*, and *Frommer's 500 Extraordinary Islands*. New York City makes a convenient jumping-off point for her travels with her husband and three children. Check out her website at www.hollyahughes.net.

An Invitation to the Reader

In researching this book, we discovered many wonderful places—hotels, restaurants, shops, and more. We're sure you'll find others. Please tell us about them, so we can share the information with your fellow travelers in upcoming editions. If you were disappointed with a recommendation, we'd love to know that, too. Please write to:

Frommer's 100 Best Beaches, 1st Edition
John Wiley & Sons, Inc. • 111 River St. • Hoboken, NJ 07030-5774
frommersfeedback@wiley.com

An Additional Note

Travel information can change quickly and unexpectedly, and we strongly advise you to confirm important details locally before traveling, including information on visas, health and safety, traffic and transport, accommodations, shopping, and eating out. We also encourage you to stay alert while traveling and to remain aware of your surroundings. Avoid civil disturbances, and keep a close eye on cameras, purses, wallets, and other valuables.

While we have endeavored to ensure that the information contained within this guide is accurate and up-to-date at the time of publication, we make no representations or warranties with respect to the accuracy or completeness of the contents of this work and specifically disclaim all warranties, including without limitation, warranties of fitness for a particular purpose. We accept no responsibility or liability for any inaccuracy or errors or omissions, or for any inconvenience, loss, damage, costs, or expenses of any nature whatsoever incurred or suffered by anyone as a result of any advice or information contained in this guide.

The inclusion of a company, organization, or website in this guide as a service provider and/or potential source of further information does not mean that we endorse them or the information they provide. Be aware that information provided through some websites may be unreliable and can change without notice. Neither the publisher nor authors shall be liable for any damages arising herefrom.

Frommer's Icons

We use four feature icons to help you quickly find the information you're looking for. At the end of each review, look for:

 Where to get more information

✈ Nearest airport

 Nearest train station

🛏 Recommended kid-friendly hotels

Frommers.com

Frommer's travel resources don't end with this guide. Frommer's website, www.frommers.com, has travel information on more than 4,000 destinations. We update features regularly, giving you access to the most current trip-planning information and the best airfare, lodging, and car-rental bargains. You can also listen to podcasts, connect with other Frommers.com members through our active-reader forums, share your travel photos, read blogs from guidebook editors and fellow travelers, and much more.

Why These 100 Beaches?

There's something powerful about standing at water's edge, with your toes digging into the sand, feeling the primal pull of the sea and gazing out to a vast sweep of endless sky. Whether or not you think of yourself as a "beach person" almost doesn't matter. Maybe it's only one afternoon out of your vacation; maybe it's the whole focus of your vacation; maybe your entire life is organized around logging as much beach time as possible. However it works for you, a beautiful beach can restore your spirits in ways you may not have even known you needed.

Of course, there's no one-size-fits-all formula for the dream beach vacation. One person wants calm shallow waters; a sportier type may prefer lively winds and rolling surf. One couple needs to amuse a contingent of the sandpail set; another couple desires a secluded, relaxing romantic getaway. One traveler seeks a silent, mystical communion with wild sand and sea; another craves margaritas on the sand and a nonstop disco beat. Rest assured: We've got something here for every taste.

With this book, we've tried to give you a sampling of top-notch beach vacations, all across the United States and around the world as well. Beyond singing their praises—and, frankly, these beaches are all supremely easy to sell—we'll share nuggets of history and natural history that will deepen your appreciation. And we'll help you make the most of your beach adventures, with insider advice on the best season to go, the prime times of day, the easiest ways to get there, and what gear you'll need and where to get it.

You'll find at the end of every write-up useful information about informational websites, transportation options, and **hotel recommendations.** While we didn't have space for full reviews, these choices are solid values conveniently located close to the beach. The three **price ranges** noted— $$$ (expensive), $$ (moderate), and $ (inexpensive)—are all relative to the local market. A $125-per-night motel room on an out-of-the-way island might seem expensive, but if you can find something clean and safe at that price in Miami, snap it up. For fuller descriptions (and other useful travel info), please consult the corresponding Frommer's guides for these destinations or log onto Frommers.com.

Note that any **phone numbers** listed are what you'd dial from the United States—for local dialing, skip the country code and add a 0 before the first number.

Waikiki Beach
The Key to Waikiki
Oahu, Hawaii, U.S.A.

CUE UP THE HAWAII FIVE-O THEME SONG. LINED WITH HIGH-RISE hotels and posh shopping malls, famous Waikiki Beach is like a 1960s dream of a beach vacation, with every hotel room only a few steps from a crescent of glorious pink sand with a long rolling surf break.

Set on Oahu's southern coast, the beach at Waikiki (the name means "spouting waters" in Hawaiian) was famous long before Hawaii won statehood in 1959. Hawaiian royalty once relaxed here in an immense coconut grove (now the Royal Hawaiian shopping center, 2201 Kalakua Ave.). At the end of what is now Liliokalani

Waikiki Beach.

Avenue you'll see the mystical **Wizard Stones,** four gigantic basalt boulders that tradition claims were endowed with special *mana* (spiritual power) by ancient Polynesian healers. In 1877 King David Kalakaua—perhaps foreseeing the future—set aside 140 acres (57 hectares) of prime real estate at the beach's eastern end as a park; today **Kapiolani Park** (named for his wife) is a welcome oasis of spreading banyans, huge monkeypod trees, and royal poincianas, containing the 42-acre (17-hectare) **Honolulu Zoo.** In the 1890s, the Sans Souci guest house welcomed such visitors as English writer Robert Louis Stevenson; in 1901, the sprawling Moana Surf-rider hotel followed, the granddaddy of Waikiki Beach hotels. By 1904, visitors were being enticed to ride Honolulu's new trolley line to one of the world's first public aquariums, the excellent **Honolulu Aquarium** (2777 Kalakua Ave., across from Kapiolani Park). From 1912 through the 1960s, Olympic swimming champion Duke Kahanamoku popularized world-wide the traditional Hawaiian sport of surfing, which he learned as a boy on Waikiki Beach. (Look for his lei-draped bronze statue near the Wizard Stones.)

But with statehood in 1959, Waikiki Beach really boomed, giving it the sleek urban profile it has today. The first high-rise, the Ilikai Hotel, went up in 1964; it's featured in the opening credits of *Hawaii Five-O*, which debuted in 1968 and further fuelled Waikiki's popularity. More high-rises followed, ensuring that every inch of beachfront would be occupied. Somewhat belatedly perhaps, in recent years zoning battles have been waged to require beach-front setback and limit hotels' height.

While gorgeous resort areas have since been developed throughout the islands, Waikiki is still Hawaii's premiere beach, attracting nearly five million visitors a year to its calm shallow waters and surf-ready waves. Beachgoers lounge towel-to-towel on this fairly short beach—only 1½ miles (2.4km), with half of it marked off for surfers. (Hire one of the famous Waikiki beach boys for a surfing lesson or outrigger canoe excursion.) Waikiki Beach proper runs in front of the Royal Hawaiian Hotel and the Moana Surfrider; the tranquil waters of wall-sheltered **Kuhio Beach** continue along Kalakaua Avenue to Kapahulu Pier. Southeast of the pier, the crowds lessen at **Queen's Surf,** popular with gay tourists, and calm **Sans Souci Beach,** nicknamed "Dig Me" beach by the locals because of all the tanned beauties strutting their stuff.

(i) www.visit-oahu.com.

✈ Honolulu International.

🛏 $$$ **Royal Hawaiian,** 2259 Kalakaua Ave., Waikiki (© **808/ 923-4620** or 808/923-7311; www.royal-hawaiian.com). $$ **Waikiki Parc,** 2233 Helumoa Rd. (© **800/422-0450** or 808/921-7272; www.waikikiparchotel.com).

The Classics

Cape May

The Real Jersey Shore

New Jersey, U.S.A.

YOU MAY THINK YOU KNOW THE JERSEY SHORE FROM THE TV SERIES *Jersey Shore*—but the escapades of Snooki, JWow, and the Situation don't tell the whole story. Southern New Jersey's Atlantic coast encompasses everything from glitzy Atlantic City to Bruce Springsteen's old stomping grounds in gritty Asbury Park—and at the very southern tip, the place where it all started: America's oldest vacation resort, Cape May.

A spit of land dividing Delaware Bay from the Atlantic Ocean, Cape May was first discovered by Dutch sea captain Cornelius Jacobsen Mey in 1620, the same year the Pilgrims landed at Plymouth Rock. By 1761 wealthy Philadelphians were fleeing the summer swelter at breezy Cape May; over the years such visitors as Abraham Lincoln, Robert E. Lee, and P.T. Barnum summered in its seaside inns. Forced to rebuild after a devastating 1878 fire, Cape May rose again like a phoenix, building a new town in the prevailing ornate Victorian style. Cape May's gingerbread cottages and gabled mansions create such a stunning period ensemble; in 1976 the entire town was named a National Historic Landmark.

Since World War II, Cape May has been an island, divided from mainland New Jersey by a defensive canal. Luckily, the postwar tourist boom that overdeveloped the Jersey Shore didn't cross the

canal, leaving Cape May's Victorian streetscapes beautifully intact. Cape May draws three kinds of visitors: Couples seeking quaint romantic B&Bs; families ensconced in affordable beachfront motels; and birdwatchers intent on watching spring and fall migrations at the Cape May Migratory Bird Refuge (Sunset Blvd.).

Cape May is compact enough that you can park your car at your hotel and get around town via bicycle, four-wheeled surrey, or horse-drawn carriage tours. The most important street to know is **Beach Drive,** which runs the length of Cape May's beautiful public town beach. Locals know which sections of beach to head for—the **Cove** for families, **Broadway** and **Steger's Beach** for teenagers and young adults, **Poverty Beach** for peace and quiet, and **Congress Street** for the Congress Hall hotel's beach chair and towel service. Many beachgoers just pick the section nearest their favorite restaurants or bars. Concessions and public restrooms are located along the 2-mile (3km) paved Promenade. In summer, your inn or motel should supply you with the required town beach tag.

For sunset watching, follow Sunset Boulevard west to **Sunset Beach** on the bay side of Cape May Point—it has a nice swimming cove, easy parking, and a beach grill. Some other outlying beaches are great for beachcombing (no swimming): Try **Higbee Wildlife Management Area** on the bay side (take New England Avenue), or **Cape May Point State Park** (Lighthouse Avenue), where you can climb up the **Cape May Lighthouse** (www.capemaymac.org), the second-tallest operating lighthouse in the United States. It's a grueling (and narrow) climb of 199 steps, but your reward will be breathtaking views of ocean, bay, and shoreline.

ⓘ www.capemay.com.

✈ Newark (150 miles/241km) or Baltimore (159 miles/256km).

🛏 $$$ **The Star Inn,** 29 Perry St. (✆ **800/297-3779;** www.thestarinn.net). $$ **Montreal Inn,** Beach at Madison Ave. (✆ **800/525-7011** or 609/884-7011; www.montreal-inn.com).

Galveston Island
Texas Time-Warp
Texas, U.S.A.

TALK ABOUT COLORFUL HISTORIES—GALVESTON ISLAND WAS FOUNDED by a pirate (Jean Lafitte, who based his "pirate kingdom" here in 1817) and became a den of bootlegging and gambling during Prohibition. It has definitely had its moments of glory, too—in the later 19th century this long 32-mile-long (51km) barrier island was Texas's leading port and biggest city, its downtown known as the "Wall Street of the Southwest."

But Galveston has also known tragedy. Its darkest moment came on September 8, 1900, when 20-ft-high (6m) waves crashed over low-lying Galveston in the middle of the night, smashing one-third of its houses and drowning 6,000 residents. It still ranks as the deadliest natural disaster in U.S. history (get the full story in the film *The Great Storm* at Galveston's **Pier 21 Theater**).Galveston valiantly rebuilt, erecting a stout 10-mile-long (16km) seawall and raising the entire island with landfill, yet most businesses relocated to inland Houston, and Galveston spun into a decades-long decline.

Ironically, that long decline had a silver lining. With real-estate development at a standstill, nobody knocked down the gracious Victorian mansions of the East End (north of Broadway, from 9th to 19th streets.) or the ornate cast-iron facades of the old **Strand District** (19th to 25th sts. between Church Street and the harbor). In the 1960s and 1970s a historic restoration movement rescued hundreds of dilapidated gems; walking around these districts today is a time-warp experience. Three magnificent East End houses, known as the Broadway Beauties, were opened to the public: the castle-like stone **Bishop's Palace** (1402 Broadway); the Italianate red-brick **Ashton Villa** (2328 Broadway); and the opulent brick-and-limestone 1895 **Moody Mansion** (2618 Broadway). The jewelbox **1894 Grand Opera House** (2020 Postoffice St.) again hosts live theater.

Resurgent Galveston has become a popular weekend getaway for Texans; many Houstonians can be here in an hour or less, cruising over a causeway from the mainland. Facing onto the Gulf of Mexico, the smooth brown sands and warm waters of **Stewart Beach** (6th Street and Seawall Boulevard) and **East Beach** (1923 Boddeker Dr.) are packed on summer weekends. Operated by the city, they have restrooms and outdoor showers; parking fees apply. Stewart Beach, closer to town, is more family-oriented, with beach volleyball and a snack bar. Wide open East Beach is known as a party beach, with live music and sandcastle competitions.

Galveston's most recent disaster, 2008's Hurricane Ike, damaged many of the historic district's cast-iron facades, but Stewart Beach and East Beach escaped relatively unscathed. The more undeveloped beaches on the windswept west end of the island didn't fare as well, but thanks to the volunteer clean-up efforts of devoted parkgoers, **Galveston Island State Park** (Seawall Boulevard., 14901 FM 3005; www.tpwd.state.tx.us) was back in operation within six months after Ike. Galveston has a history of overcoming disaster—it's sure to spring back better than ever.

ⓘ www.galveston.com.

✈ Galveston.

🛏 $$ **Harbor House**, #8 Pier 21 (𝄞 **800/874-3721** or 409/763-3321; www.harborhousepier21.com). $$$ **Hotel Galvez**, 2024 Seawall Blvd. (𝄞 **877/999-3223** or 409/765-7721; www.wyndham.com).

4 The Classics

Newport Beach
Balboa Beach Ball
California, U.S.A.

ON THE FOURTH OF JULY, 1906, NEARLY 1,000 DAY-TRIPPERS crowded onto electric railcars, dressed in their best beachwear—long dresses, brimmed hats, and parasols for the women, suits and straw boaters for the men. It took an hour to putter 50 miles (80km)

Having a blast in the Fun Zone.

south from Los Angeles, but when they got there, they marveled at the rail-line's new terminus: a long fishing pier over the Pacific Ocean, and, sitting on pilings in Newport Bay (newly dredged from a marshy estuary), the jaunty cupola-topped Balboa Pavilion. Built in just 10 days, it was a mad gamble by land developers, hoping to sell house lots on this heretofore empty spit of sand.

The gamble paid off. Newport Beach's real estate is now some of the most expensive property in the country, especially on the man-made islands developers located around Newport Bay, today an immense yacht-filled harbor. (Take the tiny three-car auto ferry from Palm Street over to residential **Balboa Island,** its million-dollar cottages packed onto tiny lots.) This is the posh face of Southern California, as seen in the TV series *The OC*—posh but not exclusive, for anyone can drop a towel on Newport Beach's 10 miles (16km) of golden sands, cited as one of the U.S.'s cleanest beaches. Half of that is located right on the coast-hugging Balboa peninsula; other beaches include roomy Corona del Mar State Beach and Crystal Cove State Beach to the south.

Like its counterparts up the coast, Santa Monica **24** and Santa Cruz **71**, the **Balboa Pavilion** (www.balboapavilion.com) preserves the spirit of California's early era of seaside amusements. In its day, it has hosted everything from 1920s bathing beauty parades to Depression-era dance marathons (the Balboa Shuffle dance step was all the rage) to 1950s bowling tournaments to a 1960s art museum. In 1936, it was joined by the outdoor rides of the **Fun Zone** (www. thebalboafunzone.com), west of the Pavilion between Palm Avenue and Main Street. Today you can sit in the Pavilion's **Harborside Restaurant** and watch a stream of pleasure boats at the dock—

harbor cruises, whale-watching tours, sport-fishing excursions, the high-speed catamaran to lovely Catalina Island. At night, the Pavilion's Victorian silhouette, lit with 1,500 electric bulbs, shines a welcome across the harbor.

Meanwhile, over on the Pacific side of the peninsula, cyclists, rollerbladers, and joggers join pedestrians on a concrete promenade coursing for nearly 3 miles (4.5km) along sparkling **Ocean Front Beach,** from 36th street to F street. Along its route, you'll pass the **Newport Pier** at 21st street (where the Dory Fishing Fleet's captains sell freshly caught fish every morning) and **Balboa Pier** across from the Pavilion at Main Street. Each pier has a water-view restaurant at the end, but otherwise they are wide open for quiet ocean-gazing and fishing. At low tide, check out the pilings of Balboa Pier—they're covered with clinging starfish, who feed on the large population of mussels in these waters. Real-estate developers may have manufactured many of Newport Beach's charms, but nature still peeks through.

ⓘ www.newportbeach-cvb.com, www.visitnewportbeach.com.

✈ John Wayne Airport (Santa Ana).

🛏 $$ **Bay Shores Peninsula Hotel,** 1800 W. Balboa Blvd. (ⓒ **800/222-6675** or 949/675-3463; www.thebestinn.com). $$ **Best Western Newport Beach Inn**, 6208 West Coast Hwy. (ⓒ **800/523-5549** or 949/642-8252; www.bestwestern.com).

The Classics

Cooper's Beach
Hanging in the Hamptons
Southampton, New York, U.S.A.

NAVIGATING THE HAMPTONS IS NOT EASY FOR OUTSIDERS. TO BEGIN with, the names of these tony eastern Long Island towns are confusingly similar—Westhampton, Southampton, Bridgehampton, East Hampton (***Note:*** It's *not* spelled Easthampton)—but you also have to know the Native American town names in between, like Quogue, Sagaponack, Montauk, and Amagansett. Power brokers, media moguls, and titans of finance reside in stunning mansions hidden behind high hedges, and mingle in an exclusive sphere of country clubs, charity events, and polo games. Route 27, which connects the towns, slows to a maddening crawl on summer weekends; getting a reservation at this season's "hot" restaurants is an art in itself.

In the Hamptons, insider knowledge is necessary even to go to the beach. Take Southampton Village, for example—a separately incorporated part of Southampton Town (see how confusing it gets?), founded in 1640 and the first English settlement in New York State. Lovely Southampton Village has nearly 7 miles (11km) of fine public beaches, a continuous strip of sparkling dunes, clear blue ponds, and incredibly soft white sand. Yet almost every beach's parking lot requires a town sticker, or charges daily parking fees. And at Southampton's main beach, Cooper's Beach, that fee is a whopping $40.

So what makes Cooper's Beach worth $40? (Besides the snack pavilion, rest rooms, shower, umbrella rentals, and lifeguards, that is.) Why did it win the top spot on Dr. Beach's (aka Dr. Stephen Leatherman) prestigious Best U.S. Beaches list in 2010? With its fringing shade trees, sparkling clean sand, and clear, calm water, it's truly beautiful, and great for swimming. And as a bonus, you get not only ocean views but a peek at magnificent beachfront mansions. Since all of Southampton's beaches are public, those bold-face-name residents may be joining you on the sand.

So here are a few insider tips. Avoid the parking issue by walking or biking to the beach; or stay at a hotel that gives its guests town beach parking rights. Note that parking lots fill up early, often before noon, but parking space is deliberately limited—even when lots are full, the beach may not be too crowded. The biggest crowds will be right by the Cooper's Beach parking lot, so enter instead at another of Southampton's 11 beach access points (try streets like Fowler, Old Town, Wyandanch, Gin Lane, or Cryder), and then walk along the sand to an uncrowded spot—all the beaches are connected, and they're all extraordinarily beautiful.

If watersports are your thing, you'll have other destinations—the breezy bays lying behind the barrier beaches (Tiana,

Shinnecock, Peconic, and Noyac Bays) for windsurfing, or the big waves and tricky currents out east at Montauk for surfing. Hanging out with the rich and famous, though—that's the real sport of summers in the Hamptons.

✈ John F. Kennedy International (98 miles/158km) or LaGuardia (91 miles/146km), New York City.

🛏 $$$ **Southampton Inn,** 91 Hill St., Southampton (✆ **800/832-6500** or 631/283-6500; www.southamptoninn.com). $$$ **Seatuck Cove House,** 61 S. Bay Ave., Eastport (✆ **631/325-3300;** www.seatuckcovehouse.com).

6 The Classics

Miami Beach
Rat Pack Redux
Florida, U.S.A.

IN THE LATE 1950S AND EARLY 1960S, MIAMI BEACH SEEMED THE epitome of vacation glamour—America's Riviera, haunt of the Rat Pack, showman Jackie Gleason, and mobster Al Capone. Its long strip of barrier beach boasted massive resort hotels with fantasy architecture as exotic as their names (Eden Roc, Fontainebleau). When cheap airfares made overseas destinations—including the real Riviera—more available, Miami Beach's glory faded, only to roar back, phoenix-like, in the 1980s with the renaissance of formerly dowdy South Beach and its Art Deco hotels. If Miami Beach was hot at mid-century, by the dawn of the 21st century it was white hot.

Officially distinct from mainland Miami—that great multicultural stewpot across Biscayne Bay—stylish Miami Beach is a separately incorporated city, tethered to the mainland by half a dozen causeways. Its spine, Collins Avenue, fronts 12 miles (19km) of wide, well-maintained white-sand beach and blue-green waters from 1st to 86th streets; that strand continues north of Miami Beach proper, spooling through Surfside, ritzy Bal Harbour, and the adjacent barrier islands, the Sunny Isles, adding up to some 35 miles (56km) of beach. Although most of this stretch is lined with hotels and condos, there's plenty of public access to that hard-packed white-sand beach. It's definitely an urban beach, with periodic lifeguard stands and restrooms, a wooden boardwalk runs from 21st to 46th streets, enabling visitors to get a taste of the beach without getting sand in their shoes.

Miami Beach.

That fabulous beach spawned Miami Beach, but nowadays beachcombing is beside the point. Lovely (and pricey) as those pastel-hued SoBe boutique hotels are, their rooms are often also tiny and minimally furnished. Hanging out in hip South Beach is all about seeing and being seen, with everyone from rock stars and fashion icons to club kids and trannies flocking to the bars, restaurants, and poolside lounges. (The beach may be public, but those elegant beachfront hotels all seem to have their own stylish pools as well, which are strictly for hotel guests only.) Most night-lifers hop from bar to bar throughout the evening; perennial favorite haunts are the **Rose Bar** at the Delano Hotel (1685 Collins Ave.), the **SkyBar** at the Shore Club (1901 Collins Ave.), and the retro **Martini Bar** at the Raleigh Hotel (1775 Collins Ave.). Collins and Washington avenues are the eye of the storm, but be forewarned: the scene doesn't even begin to buzz until 11pm.

Where there are fashionistas, there will be luxe shopping, and **Collins Avenue** has become Miami's designer-laden equivalent of Madison Avenue. The **Lincoln Road pedestrian mall,** originally designed in 1957 by Morris Lapidus, is a little more low-rent and, frankly, more fun. If you must have your Rodeo Drive experience, head north to Bal Harbour, where the exclusive **Bal Harbour Shops** mall can put a dent in your credit cards.

ⓘ www.miamibeachfl.gov.

✈ Miami International Airport or Fort Lauderdale Hollywood International Airport.

🛏 $$ **Circa 39 Hotel,** 3900 Collins Ave. (ⓒ **877/824-7223** or 305/538-4900; www.circa39.com). $$ **South Seas Hotel,** 1751 Collins Ave. (ⓒ **800/345-2678** or 305/205-6195; www.southseas hotel.com).

The Classics

7

Biarritz
Puttin' on the Ritz
France

"CHILL THE CHAMPAGNE, PACK THE PEARLS, AND TUNE UP THE Bugatti." Thus did the Duke and Duchess of Windsor—aka the abdicated English king Edward VIII and his scandalous divorcee bride Wallis Simpson—issue orders to the servants for a spin down to the posh French seaside resort of Biarritz.

Fabulous as the French Riviera may be, it's a newcomer compared to Biarritz. Down on the southwest coast—which locals declare isn't really France, but Basque country—this former whaling town became the favorite retreat of European aristocrats in the mid-19th century, when Napoleon III and his wife, the Spanish-born Empress Eugénie, first began to vacation here. The exuberant Beaux-Arts villa that Napoleon III built for Eugénie still stands, only now it's the grand **Hôtel du Palais** (1 Av. de l'Impératrice). Before the Revolution of 1917, so many Russian nobles summered

Biarritz.

here, they built an ornate Byzantine-style **Russian Orthodox church** across from the Hôtel du Palais. The British royal family—first Queen Victoria, then her son Edward VII—were regulars as well. In 1901, the opening of the sleek Art Deco **Casino Barriére** (1 av. Edouard-VII) moved refined Biarritz into a new era as a luxury playground for a racy social set of Smart Young Things. Everyone from Cole Porter to Ernest Hemingway to Frank Sinatra came here to drink, dance, and carry on affairs—a sort of pre-jet jet set.

At the heart of it all is the **Grande Plage,** Biarritz's broad golden beach, with its rolling surf and dramatic offshore rocks. In the Victorian era, ladies promenaded this beach under parasols and wide-brimmed veiled hats; today, some bathers don't even wear tops. It's a crowded but fascinating scene at the height of the winter season, though Biarritz stays busy year-round. The paved promenade **Quai de la Grande Plage** runs along the beach, from the beachfront Casino south to gracious place Ste-Eugénie, a great place for an early evening rendezvous. Nightlife buzzes in the old fishing port area, **Port des Pêcheurs,** south of the Grand Plage.

North of the Hôtel de Palais, the broad sands continue with **Plage Miramar.** Families prefer the placid waters of small, horse-shoe-shaped **Plage du Port-Vieux,** south of the Port des Pêcheurs. Even farther south of the town center, Boulevard du Prince de Galles leads to **Plage de la Côte des Basques,** where crashing breakers have made Biarritz a 21st-century hotspot of another kind—one of the world's top surfing destinations.

Set on the Atlantic rather than the more tranquil Mediterranean, Biarritz has always made the most of its sensational ocean panorama—crashing waves, hulking rocks, a slim white lighthouse on the headlands north of town. Near the Port des Pêcheurs, you can cross a perilous-looking footbridge—designed by no less than Gustave Eiffel—to the wave-pounded **Rocher de la Vierge** (Rock of the Virgin) for truly breathtaking 360-degree coastal views. On a clear day you can even see the mountains of Spain.

ⓘ www.biarritz.fr.

✈ Biarritz/Anglet/ Bayonne Airport.

🛏 $$$ **Hôtel du Palais,** 1 Av. de l'Imperatrice (ⓒ **800/223-6800** or 33/5/59 41 64 00; www.hotel-du-palais.com). $ **Hôtel Atalaye,** 6 rue des Goelands, Plateau de l'Atalaye (ⓒ **33/5/59 24 06 76;** www.hotelatalaye.com).

8 **The Classics**

The Lido Di Venezia
The Lido Shuffle
Venice, Italy

THERE ARE ISLANDS ALL AROUND VENICE; VENICE ITSELF IS AN ISLAND, or rather a huddled mass of islands. There's water *everywhere*. Nevertheless, when the Venetians themselves want a day by the sea, there's only one place to go: The Lido.

Centuries ago, the Doge's navy sailed out from this long, thin barrier island, which separates the Venetian lagoon from the Gulf of Venice, an arm of the Adriatic Sea. Nowadays it's easily reached by the ACTV waterbus—there's a direct boat from the train station (# 35), and the #1 vaporetto also sails over once it's finished cruising the Grand Canal. You'll arrive on the lagoon side of the island, with its shady waterside promenade. This island also has several residential neighborhoods, but on a summer's day the passengers will mostly be heading one direction: Down the **Gran Viale,** which leads from the waterbus landing across the island to the Lido's 18km-long (11-mile) sandy sloping beach.

The public sections of the Lido beach—along Lungomare G. D'Annunzio—are a wonderfully egalitarian hangout, with lots of families, although you can also expect a few topless sunbathers and men in skimpy Speedos. The broad strip of silvery sand is convivially crowded; you can combine sunbathing with people-watching. Protected by a system of outlying dikes, the waters lapping the beach are calm and shallow, great for youngsters, and almost ridiculously warm, practically like a bathtub. The bottom's a little sludgy, but blessedly free of rocks or sharp shells.

The Lido wears a more aristocratic face down along palm-lined **Lungomare Marconi,** where you'll find two sister bastions of Old World resort elegance, the **Hotel des Bains** and the **Hotel Excelsior.** In the 1920s, when the Lido was the most fashionable strand in Italy, these *grande dame* hotels hosted a revolving crowd of international aristocrats, a milieu that the great German novelist Thomas Mann captured in *Death in Venice.* Italian director Luciano Visconti shot his 1971 film of that classic novel here; you may also recognize it from scenes in the 2006 James Bond film *Casino Royale.* The wedding-cake-like Hotel des Bains is now an exclusive residential complex, but the Excelsior, with its fanciful red Moorish-style architecture, still hosts guests. The meticulously groomed private beaches of both properties feature elegant white canvas beach huts for swimmers, as well as private pools and watersports equipment.

Note that hotel space is at a premium every September, when the Lido is a hive of activity during the **Venice Film Festival.** Several events take place at the 1930s-Modernist Palazzo del Cinema and the adjacent Art Deco Casino.

(i) www.turismovenezia.it.

✈ Aeroporto Marco Polo.

🛏 $$$ **Hotel Excelsior,** Lungomare Marconi 41, Lido (✆ **39/41/526-0201;** www.hotelexcelsiorvenezia.com). $$ **Hotel Rivamare,** Lungomare Marconi 44, Lido (✆ **39/41/526-0352;** www.hotelrivamare.com).

---

9   **The Classics**

Bora Bora
Do the Lagoon Swoon
French Polynesia

THIS IS THE LANDSCAPE OF YOUR EVERY TROPICAL-ISLAND FANTASY: Lush South Seas mountains slope down to a lagoon brocaded with swirls of sapphire-blue and neon-turquoise water. Palm-fringed atolls and coral reefs border the lagoon, enclosing its crystalline waters around nearly the entire island. Set upon those lagoon-fringing islets, or motus, luxe resorts house guests in thatched over-water bungalows, where you sleep at night completely surrounded by the murmur of tropical seas.

Nothing says "ultimate honeymoon" quite like Bora Bora. This French Polynesian island's extraordinary natural beauty has been trumpeted for years in glossy brochures, so perhaps it's not surprising that most vacationers here are starry-eyed newlyweds, splurging on a once-in-a-lifetime exotic escape. But this fabled destination is also remote enough—and expensive enough—that it will never draw huge tourist crowds. Bora Bora's luxurious mystique will remain intact.

Even the most jaded globe-trotters gasp in wonder at Bora Bora's postcard-perfect lagoon, with the basalt silhouette of **Mount Otemanu** crowning the main island in the background. And many visitors never get farther than that idyllic tableau. They stick to their own love-nests-on-stilts, stroll along boardwalk walkways to their resort's romantic restaurant, and sign up for watersports on the sandy-bottomed lagoon. Shark feeding is the signature activity, but the snorkeling and scuba diving here are world-class. Guests cruise the lagoon in all sorts of watercraft—light sea-kayaks; Polynesian-style outrigger canoes; and glass-bottom boats that allow you to stare deep into the lagoon, perhaps sighting a manta ray, green turtles, or colorful clownfish. Sunset sailing tours circle the island on swift catamarans, with Tahitian singers and dancers entertaining on board. Most resorts also provide regular shuttle boat service to the airport or to the main town of Vaitape.

With all this aqua-centered activity, it's surprising to learn that Bora Bora has few public beaches. Most resort motus have their own private white-sand beaches (many have fabulously land-scaped swimming pools as well, or even individual plunge pools in each villa). To get out of the resort bubble, head to the main island's splendid **Matira Beach** (keep to the road that starts at Hotel Bora Bora and make your way southeast toward Matira Point, at the southern end of the island). Several private homes have been built on the other side of the road, but the beach itself is still remarkably undeveloped. You can hike for 3km (1¾ miles) along Rofau Bay, shaded by tall coconut palms, where nothing but powdery white sand lies between you and the lagoon's shallow, sun-dappled water.

Whatever you do on Bora Bora, there is one place you must visit before you fly back home: **Bloody Mary's** (Povai Bay). Part barbecue fish joint, part island watering hole, this beloved spot incorporates Polynesian décor elements to great effect, from the thatched-roof dining room to the sugary-sand floor (you eat barefoot), with rustic tables and stools made of coconut palm wood. It's like a *South Pacific* fantasy—except it's real.

ⓘ www.tahiti-tourisme.com.

✈ Bora Bora-Motu Mute (connections to Tahiti, Moorea, Huahine, and Raiatea).

🛏 $$$ **Four Seasons Bora Bora,** Motu Tehotu (✆ **689/603130;** www.fourseasons.com/borabora). $$ **Le Maitai,** Matira Point (✆ **689/603000;** www.hotelmaitai.com).

10

Corfu
Worth an Odyssey
Greece

IN ONE OF THE WORLD'S FIRST TRAVEL GUIDES, THE ODYSSEY, THE Greek poet Homer wrote of his hero Odysseus washing up on the enchanting shores of Corfu. Greek mythology's other great sea-traveler, Jason, was said to have landed here with his Argonauts. And for roughly 4 centuries, the great seafaring Venetian Empire ruled this Ionian island, building a neoclassical seaport city so beautiful, it's now a World Heritage site.

Corfu has been a desirable travel destination since time immemorial. It's still popular, though all too many of today's visitors come on quick package tours or brief cruise stops. Corfu deserves so much more.

Corfu—or, to call it by its Greek name, Kerkyra—is the largest and northernmost of the Ionian islands, which hug Greece's west coast just across the Adriatic Sea from Italy's boot-heel. Mention the words "Greek island" and most people visualize rocky hillsides covered with fragrant arid scrub; Corfu is a different thing altogether, a verdant wildflower-carpeted landscape of olive, fig, and lemon trees, grapes, and pomegranates. (Thanks to the Venetians' olive oil industry, today Corfu holds some five million olive trees.) The weather is so temperate—subtropical, even—that banana trees thrive in spots.

But one thing Corfu does have in common with those other Greek islands: beautiful beaches for visitors to relax upon. The most popular is **Paleokastritsa,** on the west coast, three scallops of white sand along emerald-green bays enclosed by cave-riddled cliffs. If this gorgeous scene looks familiar, that may be because it was a location for the 1981 James Bond movie *For Your Eyes Only,*

19

which was filmed all over Corfu. South of Paleokastritsa, there's another sparkling Blue Flag beach at **Glyfada,** a laidback resort town popular with Italian tourists. Further north on the west coast, **Agios Georgios'** fine sand and shallow water make it a great swimming spot for families. (To confuse matters, there's also an excellent flat sandy beach at another town called Agios Georgios, at the southern end of the island.) Kids also like the sweeping golden beach at **Sidari,** around the bend on the island's north end. On the northeast coast, there's excellent snorkeling in the tranquil waters off of **Kassiopi,** a vintage fishing village. South of Kassiopi, crescent-shaped **Kalami Bay** is where the Durrell family of England spent their eccentric childhood, as chronicled in Gerald Durrell's *My Family and Other Animals.* (Novelist Laurence Durrell's home is now the White House Taverna.) Although Kalami's flat beach is shingle, not sand, its clear waters make it worthy also of Blue Flag status.

While you're here, spend some time wandering the narrow historic streets of **Corfu Town,** the island's capital. Another must-see sight sits high atop Corfu in the village of Gastouri: the magnificent gardens, statuary, and neoclassical palace of **Achillion** (another shooting location for *For Your Eyes Only*). Ancient as it may look, Achillion was built in the late 1800s as a summer retreat for Empress Elizabeth of Austria—yet another of Corfu's famous visitors.

(i) http://ionian-islands.com and www.corfuonline.gr.

✈ Athens (50 min.).

⛴ From Igoumenitsou (30 min.–2 hr.) and Patras (7 hr.) in Greece, and several Italian ports, including Ancona, Bari, Brindisi, Trieste, and Venice. Check schedules and prices at www.ferries.gr.

🛏 $$ **Cavalieri,** 4 Kapodistriou St., Corfu Town (© **30/26610/39-041;** www.cavalieri-hotel.com). $$$ **Corfu Palace Hotel,** 2 Leoforos Demokratias, Corfu Town (© **30/26610/23-926;** www.corfupalace.com).

The Classics

11

Copacabana &
Ipanema Beaches
Carioca Style
Rio de Janiero, Brazil

TALL AND TAN AND YOUNG AND LOVELY / THE GIRL FROM IPANEMA *goes walking* . . . Remember Astrud Gilberto's lilting 1964 bossa nova? No ad campaign could have better conveyed the sensual allure of Rio de Janiero to listeners worldwide.

The song only mentions Ipanema, but the alluring image extends to its neighbor, Copacabana, first glamorized in the U.S. by its namesake 1940s Manhattan nightclub. Ipanema and Copacabana came into being in the 1920s, as engineers cut tunnels through the

Copacabana Beach.

mountains to give Rio de Janiero access to the Atlantic Ocean. Beaches are to Rio what cafes are to Paris, and desirable residential neighborhoods quickly blossomed behind these beautiful long crescents of white sand. The high-rises of Copacabana and Ipanema date only to the '60s and '70s, but architectural distinction is beside the point; they are THE place to live in Rio de Janiero.

Copacabana Beach, which lies closer to central Rio, is larger, running 4km (2½ miles) long, with lots of beachfront hotels; it's Rio's up-all-night outdoor party space, annually hosting New Year's Eve festivities. Ipanema's beach, at 3km (2 miles) is still sizeable, but the posh neighborhood behind it is smaller and more exclusive. Both beaches are backed by a grand beachfront boulevard—**Avenida Atlântica** along Copacabana, **Avenida Vieira Souto** along Ipanema. Both have a paved beachfront promenade as well; Copacabana's is paved in a stunning black-and-white wave motif, while Ipanema's pattern is more abstract. Both beaches get crowded in season, with lively games of volleyball, beach soccer, and *futvolei* (like volleyball, but no hands allowed), not to mention the eternal games of people-watching and flirtation. Surfers seek out the wave breaks at **Arpoador,** at Ipanema's north end, or go around the cliff face at the far end of Ipanema to **São Conrado,** also a favorite hang-gliding spot. Each beach has a specific section where gays tend to congregate: On Copacabana, the area in front of the Copacabana Palace around the Rainbow kiosk; on Ipanema, the area around Posto 8, opposite Rua Farme Amoedo.

Rio's deeply ingrained beach culture has its own time-honored etiquette. Ultra-revealing swimsuits, yes; topless sunbathing, no. Women may sit on beach chairs or towels, but men must sit directly on the sand, no matter how hot or gritty. Nobody hauls loads of equipment to the beach—food, drinks, towels, *kangas* (sarongs), and even bikinis can be bought from roving vendors once you're there. Petty thievery is common, so don't bring valuables. Beach locations are indicated by the number of the closest lifeguard station *(posta)*, numbered 1 to 11 along the two beaches. Note that many hotels have a separate entrance and elevator for beachgoers, marked ENTRADA DE BANHISTAS or ENTRADA DE SERVIÇO. Usually you can pick up a towel, chair, and/or umbrella from a window near this side entrance, returning them at the end of your sun-kissed day.

ⓘ www.ipanema.com.

✈ Rio de Janiero.

🛏 $$ Atlantis Copacabana Hotel, Rua Bulhões de Carvalho 61, Copacabana (✆ **55/21/2521-1142;** www.atlantishotel.com.br). $$$ **Praia Ipanema Hotel,** Av. Vieira Souto, Ipanema (✆ **55/21/2141-4940;** www.praiaipanema.com).

The Classics

12

Bermuda
Little Britain
Atlantic Ocean

LOOKING OUT THE PLANE WINDOW ON YOUR DESCENT INTO BERMUDA, expect to catch your breath—the waters truly are turquoise, the sands truly pink. No wonder Shakespeare was inspired to write *The Tempest* by accounts of a 1609 English shipwreck on this newly charted Atlantic island; no wonder it's an enduringly popular honeymoon destination.

Besides the honeymooners, most visitors land on Bermuda as part of a cruise itinerary; they spend a few hours on shore, then hop back on the ship and leave. What a pity. Visiting Bermuda can be like slipping into a little corner of the British Empire—albeit a balmy corner, where the policemen wear (Bermuda) shorts. Bermudans, many of whom are black descendants of African slaves, steadfastly adhere to British customs, from afternoon tea to powder-wigged judges to driving on the left. (Visitors aren't allowed to rent cars, though—you'll have to get around by taxi, motorscooter, or bike.) Bermuda became a British colony in 1620; its parliament is the oldest in the Commonwealth, and in 1995 self-governing Bermuda voted to remain a British overseas territory. With its mild climate (too cool for swimming in winter) and relatively formal resort customs, Bermuda is clearly not a hang-loose Caribbean island. Its cobblestone streets, manicured golf courses, and English-style country cottages proudly bespeak its British roots.

But there's one important difference between Britain and Bermuda: those incredible pink beaches. Many of the finest are public, with rest rooms and lifeguards, and even private hotel beaches can often be used by non-guests who eat lunch at the hotel. South Road, which traces the island's southern shore, leads to several gorgeous beaches. South of Hamilton, renowned **Elbow Beach** runs for 1.5km (1 mile) past a string of private homes and resort hotels; its safe reef-sheltered waters make it a family favorite. To the west, quiet **Astwood Cove** feels enticingly remote, secluded at the bottom of a winding road off of South Road, while popular **Warwick Long Bay**, in South Shore Park, still feels open and unspoiled, an unbroken 1km (⅔-mile) stretch of sand backed by scrubland and low grasses. Adjacent **Jobson's Cove** feels like a secret pocket beach, with shallow calm waters ideal for snorkeling. Still farther west, the long curve of **Horseshoe Bay Beach** is famously beautiful, though it's likely to be crowded if cruise ships are in port. *Tip:* Trails winding through the park nearby lead to secluded cove beaches where the cruise passengers don't go; try **Port Royal Cove** to the west, and **Peel Rock Cove** and **Wafer Rocks Beach** to the east. There's prime snorkeling off the deep pink sands of **Church Bay,** off West Side Road on Bermuda's southwestern end, while beachcombing and sunset-watching rule on the northwest end, at undeveloped and secluded **Somerset Long Bay.**

ⓘ www.bermuda.com.

✈ Bermuda International Airport, St. George's.

🛏 $$$ **Fairmont Southampton,** 101 South Rd., Southampton (✆ **866/540-4497** or 441/238-8000; www.fairmont.com). $$ **Rosemont,** 41 Rosemont Ave., Pembroke Parish (✆ **800/367-0040** or 441/292-1055; www.rosemont.bm). $$$ **Elbow Beach Hotel,** 60 South Shore Rd., Paget Parish (✆ **800/223-7434** or 441/236-3535; www.mandarinoriental.com/Bermuda).

13

Fire Island
New York's Small-Town Secret
New York, U.S.A.

FIRE ISLAND NOT ONLY HAS A PARTY SCENE, IT HAS THREE DISTINCT party scenes. Okay, so one of them has to do with backyard cook-outs and kids playing flashlight tag while their parents share wine coolers on the deck. But the other two—the raucous weekend singles scene and a notoriously hot gay party culture—truly sizzle during Fire Island's all-too-short summer season.

Fire Island is very much a summer destination; when Memorial Day hits, the hamlets fill with warm-weather revelers. The one catch: You can't get here by car, but have to take a ferry, then move around the island on foot or by bicycle, which can be a challenge, considering that this long skinny barrier island south of Long Island is only ½ mile (.8km) wide but 32 miles (51km) long. With much of the island devoted to national seashore and parkland, the housing stock is clustered in several distinct hamlets, with small houses closely packed together. (You're bound to get to know your neighbors.) Given the transportation constraints, people don't tend to stray too far from their chosen towns, so renting a Fire Island house begins with selecting the right town for your demographic.

About halfway along, **Ocean Beach** is the hub of island activity, with most of the island's hotels and restaurants, accompanied by a lively weekend singles scene. Singles also gravitate to the beach-house shares of (from west to east) Kismet, Fair Harbor, Corneille Estates, Ocean Bay Park, and Davis Park. Other towns are definitely family-oriented, prizing quiet and a 1950s-era vibe—from west to east, Saltaire, Dunewood, Atlantique, Seaview, and Point O'Woods.

Fire Island's gay social scene centers on two adjacent towns to the east of Ocean Bay Park, **Cherry Grove** and **Fire Island Pines.** The quieter community of the Pines attracts gay men, while party-central

Cherry Grove draws a crowd of women and men; the woods between Cherry Grove and the Pines, affectionately known as the "Meat Rack," host some extraordinary scenes of its own. The biggest day of the year out here is July 4th, but not for the usual patriotic reasons—that's the date of the annual Invasion of the Pines, when boatloads of drag queens from Cherry Grove come and "terrorize" the posh Pines.

There are beaches on both the north shore, fronting the Great South Bay, and the south shore, fronting on the Atlantic; each town has its own beach, sometimes two, and often a marina as well. At the far ends—near the east-end wildlife preserve of **Watch Hill,** and around the west end's historic **lighthouse**—beaches are clothing-optional, though going topless is tolerated everywhere.

ⓘ www.fireisland.com or www.nps.gov/fis.

✈ John F. Kennedy Intl (39 miles/62km); LaGuardia (48 miles/77km).

🚢 From Bay Shore to Ocean Beach/Kismet/Saltaire/Ocean Bay Park, **Fire Island Ferries** (ⓒ **631/665-3600;** www.fireisland ferries.com). From Sayville to Cherry Grove/the Pines/Sailors Haven, **Sayville Ferry** (ⓒ **631/589-0810;** www.sayvilleferry.com). From Patchogue to Davis Park, **Davis Park Ferry** (ⓒ **631/475-1665;** www.davisparkferry.com).

🛏 $$$ **Clegg's Hotel,** 478 Bayberry Walk, Ocean Beach (ⓒ **631/583-5399;** www.cleggshotel.com). $$ **Grove Hotel,** Cherry Grove (ⓒ **631/597-6600;** www.grovehotel.com).

The Party Scenes

14

Key West
Last Mango in Paradise
Florida, U.S.A.

KEY WEST IS AN ANYTHING-GOES, PARTY-HEARTY DESTINATION THAT seems the complete antithesis of the nature-oriented, family-friendly Florida Keys. And for many visitors, that's exactly why they choose Key West.

Revelers in Key West.

Old-time "conchs" (pronounced *conks*), as the locals call themselves, habitually gripe that their island paradise has been ruined. What was once a slow-paced, slightly scruffy port of call for sport fishermen and social dropouts has become overtaken with boisterous restaurants, bars, and T-shirt shops lining the heart of Old Town, **Duval Street.** Every evening, revelers grab a go-cup and crowd the docks behind **Mallory Square** for the traditional Sunset Celebration, a rowdy carnival of sketch artists, acrobats, food vendors, and other buskers (not to mention pickpockets) trading on the island's bohemian image.

But others defend Key West's live-and-let-live mentality as its greatest asset. Over the years, writers as diverse as Robert Frost, Ernest Hemingway, Tennessee Williams, and S. J. Perelman have found inspiration in its palm-shaded precincts. No one has defined the genial Key West spirit better than musician Jimmy Buffet, whose Parrothead acolytes still launch into choruses of "Margaritaville" at bars like **Sloppy Joe's** (201 Duval St.) and **Captain Tony's Saloon** (428 Green St.). The open-air **Green Parrot** (601

Whitehead St.) is another local favorite that's been pouring stiff drinks since 1890. But don't stick with just one—bar crawling is a way of life down here. At the ocean end of Duval Street, popular sandy **South Beach** is a good place to work up your thirst.

Key West's gay community has flourished since the 1970s, when many gays moved here to renovate then-dilapidated gingerbread cottages. One of America's first openly gay mayors, Richard Heyman, was elected here in the 1980's. If the straight party scene in Key West is all about drinking, the gay party scene is all about dancing. Two popular drag/disco spots are the adjacent **801 Bourbon Bar/Number One Saloon** (801 Duval St. and 514 Petronia St.); another favorite is **Aqua** (711 Duval St.). Rainbow flags flutter outside gay hangouts, nonstop dance clubs and drag performances, and a stream of same-sex couples (nowadays, several of them are officially honeymooners!) happily stroll hand in hand. You can't deny the refreshing sense of freedom at gay-magnet **Higgs Beach** or around the swimming pools at the many guesthouses with a predominantly gay clientele. Several LGBT festivals are planned throughout the year—June's PrideFest, August's Tropical Heat festival, September's WomenFest, and flamboyant FantasyFest in late October.

Ease into the mood by taking one of the town's ubiquitous sightseeing tours, themed to match various interests, by trolley, train, bike, or on foot (several are listed at www.historictours.com/keywest). Forget about bringing a car; the best way to get around Key West—which, after all, is only 2x4 miles (3.2x6.4km) and flat as a pancake—is by bicycle or moped.

ⓘ Visitor center, 1601 N. Roosevelt Blvd., ✆ **305/296-8881;** www.keywest.com.

✈ Key West or Miami International Airport (159 miles/256km).

🛏 $$ **Ambrosia Key West,** 622 Fleming St. (✆ **305/296-9838;** www.ambrosiakeywest.com). $$ **Oasis,** 822 Fleming St. (✆ **800/362-7477** or 305/296-2131; www.keywest-allmale.com).

The Party Scenes

15

Paradise Beach
The Spirit of Dionysus
Mykonos, Greece

MYKONOS IS OFTEN CALLED A GREEK ST. TROPEZ, AND FOR GOOD reason. In July and August, this Aegean island is filled to capacity with stylish 20-somethings, who party all night in Mykonos's tavernas and clubs. Boutiques stay open until 2am, catering to tipsy crowds of late-night customers. The next day, while the revelers sleep off their hangovers, the beaches are quiet until well after lunchtime.

Mykonos Old Town's beautiful whitewashed architecture attracted the likes of Jackie Kennedy and Aristotle Onassis in the '60s, and with their stamp of approval, Mykonos soon became *the* place to be for anybody who was anybody. In the hedonistic '70s, it became the island version of Studio 54, making world headlines on celebrity pages and magazines. The sheer contrast of a traditional Greek fishing village and the type of tourists it attracted— gay partiers, international jet-setters, celebrities, rock stars, and models—captured the world's imagination. While it may not be the #1 Party Capital of the Mediterranean anymore—such titles are always changing hands—it still delivers world-class nightlife for pleasure seekers of all stripes.

Mykonos greets you with its relaxed vibe as soon as you step off the ferry in Mykonos town, also known as **Chora,** a bewitching maze of whitewashed, cubic houses, where you're sure to get hopelessly lost at some point. Up on a hill behind town are the signature **windmills** emblazoned on so many Mykonos postcards. Sooner rather than later, you'll find your way to the most picturesque and popular quarter of Chora, **Little Venice,** with its stylish waterfront bars that are packed from late afternoon to sunset.

The neighborhood known as Little Venice has a popular waterfront bar scene.

Nobody around here waits for five o' clock to begin partying; watching the sunset with a drink in your hand has become an essential ritual. After dinner, you'll have to network with your fellow partiers to figure where in town this season's hot clubs and bars are, but busy **Matoyanni Street** is usually a good place to start.

The best sand beaches, and the hottest beach action, are all on the south coast. Dance music blares all day long at the two most famous beaches, **Paradise** and **Super Paradise,** where no one bats an eye at nudist sunbathing. On Paradise beach, the **Tropicana Bar** and the **Sunrise Bar** cater to a mixed crowd, and at Super Paradise, two loud bar/clubs on opposite sides of the beach cater to gay and mixed crowds, respectively. Sunset parties start around 6pm; Paradise Beach's **Paradise Club,** with its gigantic swimming pool in the middle of the club, steals the show with its nightly fireworks and a wild party that lasts until well after midnight. Meanwhile, **Cavo Paradiso Club** up the hill doesn't even get started until 2am. Hey, you can sleep on the flight home.

✈ Mykonos.

🛳 From Piraeus (4 hr.) and other Cyclades islands (45 min.–2 hr.), **Hellenic Seaways** (www.hellenicseaways.gr) and **Blue Star Ferries** (www.bluestarferries.com). Schedules and bookings at www.ferries.gr.

🛏 $$ **Argo Hotel Mykonos,** Platys Gialos 84 (© **30/22890/23405;** www.argo-mykonos.gr). $$$ **Belvedere Hotel,** School of Fine Arts District (© **30/22890/25122;** www.belvederehotel.com).

The Party Scenes

16

Ibiza
Dance to the Balearic Beat
Balearic Islands, Spain

THE HIPPIES AND PENNILESS ARTISTS WHO FIRST FELL IN LOVE WITH laidback, pleasure-loving Ibiza in the 1960s would hardly recognize the place today. This western Mediterranean island's name is now synonymous with extreme partying—it's perhaps the most legendary destination for summer revelry in Europe, probably the world.

Set in the Balearic Sea off of Spain's eastern coast, Ibiza (pronounced *ee-BEE-tha*) lies southeast of its big sister Majorca, whose popularity it has now eclipsed. Wonderfully balmy in winter, it can get steamy in summer—yet that's when most visitors come in droves. During July and August, the island is packed with middle-class Europeans on air-and-hotel package tours, but it's also a mecca for glamour girls like Kate Moss and Jade Jagger (both firm fixtures here in summer) and gays, which adds an element of chic to the alcohol- and drug-fueled madness.

Ibiza's beaches are quite beautiful—and you can have them largely to yourself in the morning and early afternoon, when most holidaymakers are still sleeping off last night's excesses. On the east coast near Santa Eulària des Riu, broad and brilliant white **Santa Eulària** is very popular, as is horseshoe-shaped **Es Cana** nearby, which has plenty of watersports and beach bars (and the old hippie market of El Canar). On the southern tip, the beach of **Playa des Cavallet** is clothing-optional and very gay-friendly.

Hit the Ibiza beaches early in the day and you'll get them largely to yourself.

The main towns on Ibiza are the Ciudad de Ibiza (often referred to as Ibiza Town, or Eivissa in the local Catalan dialect) and San Antonio. Ibiza Town's historic **Old Town,** with its cobblestoned streets, whitewashed houses, and flower-draped balconies, is a charming place to stroll, but the action is mostly down in the yacht-crowded marina area, full of art galleries, dance clubs, boutiques, bars, and restaurants. The **Montesol hotel bar** (Vara de Rey 2) is great for people-watching. Sooner or later everyone checks out the perennially hip disco **Pacha** (Av. 8 de Agosto s/n; www.pacha.com) and, out by the casino, **El Divino Club** (Puerto Ibiza Nueva, www.eldivino-ibiza.com) or immense **Disco Privilege** (Calle de Ibiza 7, San Rafael, www.privilegeibiza.com). Hotels in San Antonio, or "San An," traditionally draw the British soccer-hooligan demographic, especially in the notorious West End, so for more relaxed atmosphere, it's worth spending a bit more for a private villa on or near the beach somewhere. San An's most popular club is **Café del Mar** (www.cafedelmarmusic.com).

Whatever you do, don't show up on Ibiza in high summer without accommodations already booked. It's also worth noting that the authorities on Ibiza are not as permissive as you might expect (or hope). Drunk and disorderly conduct can lead to heavy fines and even deportation.

ⓘ www.illesbalears.es.

✈ Es Codolar International Airport, Ibiza.

🛏 $$$ **Cas Gasi,** Cami Vell a Sant Mateau, Sta. Gertrudis (𝄞 **34/971/19 77 00;** www.casgasi.com). $$ **El Hotel Pacha,** Paseo Marítimo, Ibiza Town (𝄞 **34/971/31-59-63;** www.elhotel pacha.com).

17 **The Party Scenes**

Koh Pha Ngan
Full Moon Frolic
Thailand

BEFORE BOOKING YOUR TRIP TO THAILAND, CONSULT THE LUNAR calendar—just how wild your trip will be depends on whether you hit the monthly Full Moon Party on Koh Pha Ngan. Then again, this beach-party isle in the Gulf of Thailand also has a Half-Moon Festival and Black Moon Party scheduled to celebrate other phases of the moon—a chance to party under the tropical night sky is never more than a week away.

Set on crescent-shaped Haad Rin beach on the island's southeast tip, the infamous **Full Moon Party** (http://fullmoonparty-thailand.com) is an enormous beach extravaganza that can draw upwards of 25,000 people from all over the globe for 1 night of uninhibited, unadulterated revelry. Multiple stages and sound systems blare dance music spun by the hottest DJs on the international club scene, and the cheap drinks just keep on flowing. Somewhere between the techno beats, the sideshow fire-eaters and jugglers, and impromptu fireworks displays, partygoers go for a dip in the moonlit bay. The twice-monthly **Half-Moon Festival** (www.halfmoonfestival.com) up the west coast at Baan Tai village is almost as crazy. Warning: pickpockets and unscrupulous drug dealers take full advantage of these festivals—keep your wits about you and your valuables locked in your hotel room.

Alex Garland's 1996 novel *The Beach*, about backpacker hedonism in Thailand, first put Koh Pha Ngan on the international radar; the film version of the book, released in 2000 starring Leonardo DiCaprio, sealed the deal. The island's tourism infrastructure had to grow quickly to catch up with its overnight popularity, but so far development hasn't gotten out of hand. Whereas Kho Pha Ngan was once the sole province of stoned backpackers, who crashed in hostels or slept on the beach, the island now also caters to couples and families with fully equipped resorts, many quite secluded and exclusive. Don't expect a lot of glitz and glam: Koh Pha Ngan is still ruled by the laid-back rhythms of beach life. It's a far cry from the girlie bars and karaoke lounges of over-developed Phuket, the Thai beach resort most package tourists visit there.

While those moon-centric parties are the headlining act, Koh Pha Ngan also has a wide range of perfectly relaxing activities, from bumming it on a quiet beach like **Chaloklam Bay** to snorkeling off the **Mae Haad** sandbars and diving at the coral reefs of **Koh Ma.** Local guides lead treks into the island's jungle interior, where you'll spot monkeys, wild pigs, and all manner of native birds. Yoga facilities, meditation centers, and massage treatments are also widely available—an alternative way to bliss out.

ⓘ www.kohphangan.com.

✈ Koh Samui.

🚤 From Koh Samui, about 30 min.

🛏 $$ **Drop In Club Resort,** 157/1-10 Haad Rin, Baan Tai (ⓒ **66/77/375-444;** www.dropinclubresortandspa.com). $$$ **Sarikantang,** 129/3 moo.6 Seekantang Beach, Baan Tai (ⓒ **66/77/375 055;** www.sarikantang.com).

Provincetown
Gay Pride in P-Town
Cape Cod, Massachusetts, U.S.A.

A RUSTICATED GRANITE TOWER RISES OVER THE SHINGLED ROOFS OF Provincetown, commemorating the first landfall of the Mayflower Pilgrims in 1620. Today, a different breed of pilgrims floods the narrow streets of this weathered former fishing village. According to the 2010 U.S. Census, the country's highest percentage of same-sex couples lives in Provincetown. On a bright summer weekend, it seems that all their brothers and sisters are here visiting too.

Provincetown has always embraced those whose lifestyle is a little out of the mainstream. An influx of artists and writers congregated here in the early 20th century; hippies arrived in the 1960s,

Vacationers hit the streets of lively Provincetown.

drawn to P-Town's natural beauty, bohemian vibe, and (then) cheap real-estate. Beginning in the mid-1970s, a trickle of gay men and lesbians soon grew to a steady stream. Nowadays, harborside Commercial Street seems like a gay pride parade on crowded summer days, culminating in the nonstop camp of August's Carnival weekend.

Maybe it's something in the salty Cape air, but P-Town's gay population blends seamlessly into this artsy town's broad-minded culture—raunchiness and exhibitionism seem beside the point. Plenty of other vacationers stroll these streets, taking whale watch tours and buying ice cream cones, unfazed by the bare-chested hotties relaxing on the nearest porch, or the drag queen daintily downing a lobster roll at the next table.

Most visitors, gay and straight, are also here for that stark sand-drift landscape and silvery Cape light that first attracted the artist community. Thanks to the **Cape Cod National Seashore** ㊹, which encompasses two-thirds of Provincetown, that beauty remains unspoiled. Popular P-Town sections include the rocky strand of calm **Herring Cove,** where same-sex couples congregate for sunset-watching (applauding as the sun dips into Cape Cod Bay); and surf-edged **Race Point,** where you can often spot whales swimming past.

As for night-life, there's plenty on tap, with tea-dances and piano-bar singalongs providing alternatives to frenetic dance clubs. Perhaps the nation's premier gay bar is the **Atlantic House** off Commercial Street, which also welcomes straights of both sexes (except in the leather-oriented Macho Bar upstairs). In the little bar downstairs, check out the Tennessee Williams memorabilia, including a portrait *au naturel*. The **Crown & Anchor** (247 Commercial St.) also has a number of different rooms, from a leather bar to a drag show and a disco. The drag shows at the **Post Office Café** (303 Commercial St.) are extremely popular. **Vixen** (336 Commercial St.) is probably the town's most popular women's bar. Bars close at 1am (those Massachusetts Puritan liquor laws!), when everybody ends up at **Spiritus Pizza** (150 Commercial St.) for an espresso shake.

ⓘ www.provincetown.com or www.ptown.org.

✈ Provincetown Airport.

🚢 From Boston, 90 min. or 3 hr. ⓒ **877/783-3779;** www.baystatecruisecompany.com or ⓒ 617/227-4321; www.bostonharborcruises.com.

🛏 $$$ **Carpe Diem Guesthouse and Spa,** 12-14 Johnson St. (ⓒ **800/487-0132** or 508/487-4242; www.carpediemguesthouse.com). $$ **Surfside Hotel & Suites,** 543 Commercial St. (ⓒ **860/757-8616;** www.surfsideinn.cc).

19   **The Party Scenes**

Cancun
Playing on the Playa
Mexico

EVER SINCE THE MID-1970s—WHEN MEXICAN TOURISM OFFICIALS scientifically determined that this deserted Yucatan beach area should become the Next Big Resort Destination—Cancún has delivered sand, sun, and fun to travelers from all over the world. Statistics show that more Americans travel to Cancún than to any other foreign destination; for many, it's their first time out of the country. And often that first trip to Cancún is for Spring Break, when hordes of American college students descend on the powdery sand of Cancún's beaches for a week of nonstop partying.

Cancún (which means "golden snake" in Mayan) stretches from a downtown area known as Cancún City east to Isla Cancún, aka the Hotel Zone, a narrow 15-mile (24km) barrier strip, with the turquoise Caribbean Sea sparkling on one side, the picturesque Nichupté lagoon on the other. Many visitors never leave the Hotel Zone, and why should they? The white sand beachfront is lined with massive high-rise resort hotels, but all of that beach is public—you can walk through any hotel lobby to get to its beach, and rent watersports equipment from the hotel's concessions.

Of course, many visitors choose Cancún knowing that it is the party resort in Mexico, and not just at Spring Break. The partying often begins by day at the beach, then kicks it up a notch at happy hour, when many bars along the Hotel Zone serve two-for-one drinks at sunset. Come night, the hottest centers of action are along **Kukulkán Boulevard,** which traces the length of the barrier strip. Three major nightlife complexes, **Plaza Dady'O, Forum by the Sea,** and **La Isla Shopping Village,** offer a full complement of restaurants, pubs, and dance clubs. Drinking games, DJs pumping tunes until daybreak, pool parties—this Party Central has it all. A great starter is the **Party Hopper Tour** (http://partyhoppertour.com), a bus tour that allows you to bypass the long lines at enduring hotspots like the lively terrace bar **Congo Bar** (Kukulkán Km 8.9) Señor Frog's restaurant (Kukulkán Km 9.5), and the white-hot dance club **CoCo Bongo** (Kukulkán Km 9, in Forum By the Sea). For a change of pace, head into **El Centro** to sample its salsa clubs, where you can sip tequila in a refreshing margarita or slam it with lime and salt.

While some travel purists scoff at Cancún's Americanized amenities, that ready-to-go infrastructure is a plus for many travelers, providing all the comforts of home. Direct charter flights, chain hotels, familiar menus, and plenty of English-speaking staff make it easy to forget your worries and relax on that still-stunning beach—and sometimes that's just what a vacation's for.

ⓘ www.cancun.travel or www.cancunmx.com.

✈ Cancún.

🛏 **\$\$ Bel-Air Collection Hotel & Spa,** Blvd. Kukulkán Km 20.5 (✆ **866/799-9097** or 52/998/193 1770; www.belaircancun.com). **\$\$\$ Marriott Casa Magna,** Blvd Kukulkán, Retorno Chac L-41 (✆ **888/236-2427** or 52/998/881-2000; www.marriott.com).

Punta del Este
Sunrise, Sunset
Uruguay

WEALTHY BUENOS AIREANS HAVE KNOWN ABOUT PUNTA DEL ESTE for years, snapping up vacation homes and making it their summer playground. It's taken Europeans and Americans a little longer to discover this sophisticated beach party town, with its miles of sand, luxe hotels and restaurants, and pulsating nightlife.

Some half a million people may stream through Punta del Este's resorts every summer (October through March). High season is even more specific: the two weeks after Christmas, when South America's most bronzed and beautiful take up temporary residence in its sleek pastel high-rises and beachfront homes. Secluded beaches are beside the point: Punta's revelers come here to party on public beaches, which come well stocked with bars, restaurants, and music. The challenge is to scope out where the "in crowd" is hanging out this season—it shifts from year to year.

A good place to start is **La Barra**, a beach town about 10km (6 miles) east of the main peninsula. Though it looks like a fishing village, La Barra was specifically built for tourism, and it has become Punta's nightlife nerve center. Its pubs and restaurants constantly change names; one perennial hotspot is the dance club/lounge **Tequila** (Calle 11, La Barra). Heading east from La Barra, a succession of beaches draw different crowds—**Montoya** is a surfer favorite, while the socialites patronize **Bikini** and **Manantiales.** Farther along the coastal highway, Ruta 10, sunset gatherings on upscale **Jose Ignacio Beach** are like a great country-club cocktail party.

Over on the calmer waters of Maldonado Bay, west of the peninsula, broad sandy **Playa Mansa** (Parada 1 to Parada 24) hosts lots of sports, from jet-skiing to beach soccer. Mansa's social buzz is on the rise, thanks to the new **Conrad Resort & Casino** (Parada 4, Playa Mansa), with its Vegas-style shows and torch-lit swimming pools. Farther west, 10km (6 miles) from the peninsula, rocky **Punta Ballena** is a great place for sunrise or sunset views from the modernist spires and domes of **Casapueblos,** a stunning hotel/museum that features the work of Carlos Páez Vilaró.

Punta's social whirl runs on a night-owl schedule: Many regulars begin their day with a late afternoon breakfast—try the decadent waffles at the L'Auberge hotel (Barrio Parque del Golf)—then head for a sunset party on the beach. Several glitzy boutiques on the town's chic shopping street, **Avenida Gorlero,** are only open in the evenings, and no self-respecting Punta partier would dream of making a dinner reservation any earlier than 11pm. The best parties start well after midnight and run until dawn, when rumpled partygoers, shoes in hand, stroll onto the peninsula's **Playa Brava** beach to watch the sun rise over the Atlantic—and start it all over again.

ⓘ www.vivapunta.com.

✈ Punta Del Este (45 min from Buenos Aires).

🛏 $$ **Awa Hotel,** Pedragosa Sierra and San Ciro (🕐 598/42/499999; www.awahotel.com). $$ **Best Western La Foret,** Calle la Foret, Parada 6, Playa Mansa (🕐 598/42/481-004; www.bestwestern.com).

The Party Scenes

21

Saint Tropez
For that Saint-Tropez Tan
France

ALL THE ELEMENTS WERE SPELLED OUT IN A 1980's AD CAMPAIGN: blinding sunshine, a glass of white wine, a leggy bronzed model in a skimpy black bikini. Buy Bain de Soil sun lotion, the ad suggested, and you too could have the ultimate jet-set allure—or as the jingle put it, "Bain de Soleil . . . for the Saint Tropez tan."

Party hotspots come and go, but Saint Tropez has lost none of its cachet over the years, ever since a sultry French starlet named Brigitte Bardot brought it international exposure in the late 1950s. ("Exposure" is right, given St-Trop's time-honored custom of nude sunbathing—that phrase "Saint Tropez tan" implies a full-body tan with no swimsuit lines.) Between May and September every year, the film colony, glitterati, wealthy Parisians, and a handful of artists still descend upon St-Trop's chic bars and bikini-clad beaches to see and be seen. Along that unassuming harborfront, with its jumble of modest ocher-colored buildings, million-dollar yachts vie for dock space, while fabulously expensive designer boutiques line quaint Rue François Sibilli.

Celebrities and aristocrats don't come to Saint-Tropez for seclusion—they come to preen and mingle in public, and their watering holes are well-known. By day, they congregate at the **Café de Paris** (Sur le Port) and **Café Sénéquier** (Sur le Port). When night rolls around, it's the self-consciously chic **Les Caves du Roy** (on the lobby level of the Hôtel Byblos, Avenue Paul-Signac), probably the most famous nightclub in France, or the psychedelic-themed **Le Papagayo** (in the Résidence du Nouveau-Port, rue Gambetta) and its adjacent (and expensive) **Le VIP Room.** A somewhat younger crowd gyrates at the high-tech dance club **Le Bar du Port** (Quai Suffren) or **Chez Maggy** (7 rue de Sibille). St-Trop's sizeable gay contingent gravitates to **Le Pigeonnier** (13 rue de la Ponche) and **L'Esquinade** (2 rue du Four).

For beaches, most people head south of Saint-Tropez proper to the Baie de Pampelonne, which has several small sand beaches along its 5km (3-mile) shore—a significant amenity along the Riviera, where most beaches are rocky. In this bastion of elitism, most are private beach clubs that charge an entrance fee, but for a luxe day in the sun—complete with upscale restaurants and color coordinated beach umbrellas and lounge chairs—it's a perfect St-Trop experience. The "beautiful people" favor **Plage des Salins** and **Plage des Pampelonnes;** for hedonistic exhibitionism, head to **Tahiti Beach,** on the north end of Pampelonne. Or step over the scantily clad bronzing bodies on **Coco Beach,** a favorite with gay men.

ⓘ www.ot-saint-tropez.com.

✈ Toulon-Hyeres (56km/30 miles).

🚃 St-Raphael.

🚢 From St-Raphael (50 min.).

🛏 $$ **L'hôtel Des Lices,** 135 av. Augustin-Grangeon (Ⓒ **33/ 4/94-97-28-28**; www.hoteldeslices.com). $$ **Hotel Sube,** 15 quai de Suffern (Ⓒ **33/4/94-97-30-04**; www.hotelsube.net).

Bring the Family 22

Block Island
The Word on the Block
Rhode Island, U.S.A.

ONCE UPON A TIME, BLOCK ISLAND WAS CONSIDERED A SMUGGLERS' den, a rocky, wind-whipped outpost for pirates and scavengers, huddled in the Atlantic Ocean 12 miles off the Rhode Island coast. A post-Civil War tourism boom changed all that, however, transforming Block Island into one of the country's first popular summer resorts. Even today, most visitors stay in quaint rambling Victorian-style seaside inns with rocking chairs on the front porch. You'll have a hard time convincing your kids that pirates ever hung out in this picturesque corner of New England.

Tens of thousands of summer visitors arrive on the ferry every year, yet somehow tourism hasn't spoiled the island's throwback charm. Life here moves at a relaxed pace that harried modern families appreciate. Development remains under control—you won't find any fast-food franchises or chain stores. Police officers patrol on bikes, and children tend lemonade stands in front of picket fences. There's not much point in bringing a car over on the ferry, because the island is a mere 7 miles x 3 miles wide (11km long x 5km wide); there's only one gas station, anyway. Most visitors make do with bicycles or mopeds, or call a taxi when they need to get somewhere faster.

Most of the action—and in summer it's active, indeed—is in Old Harbor, where the ferries arrive. Block Island has 17 miles (27km) of beach, but only two beaches have lifeguards, food service, and rental facilities—**Pebbly Beach,** just south of the Old Harbor's breakwater, and -long 3 miles-long (5km) **Crescent Beach,** north of Old Harbor past the Surf Hotel. Pebbly Beach is popular and often crowded, but the surf can be rough; families tend to gravitate more to Crescent Beach. In fact, Crescent's southern section is often called Kid Beach, because of its sandy bottom, shallow waters, and gentle surf. Farther along, Crescent Beach turns into a broad strand where the surf is higher; facilities include a snack bar, bathrooms, and showers, plus stands renting beach chairs, umbrellas, and boogie boards.

On a day off from the beach, consider renting bikes to explore the island—the terrain is hilly, but nothing is too far away, and there's little traffic for young riders to negotiate. Good destinations close to town are the two 19th-century lighthouses—**Southeast Lighthouse,** on Mohegan Trail, a couple miles south of Old Harbor, and **North Lighthouse,** on Corn Neck Road, north of Crescent Beach. You could also kayak around tranquil **Great Salt Pond.** Rent a kayak from Pond & Beyond (www.blockisland.com/kayakbi) or Champlin's Resort (www.champlinsresort.com), on Great Salt Pond. It's a far cry from pirate adventure, but a whole lot safer.

ⓘ Tourist office, Old Harbor ferry landing (☏ **800/383-2474;** www.blockislandchamber.com).

🚢 From Newport (2 hr.) or Point Judith (30 min. passenger ferry, 1 hr. car ferry; www.blockislandferry.com). From New London CT (1 hr. 15 min.; Block Island Express, ☏ **860/444-4624**). From Montauk NY (1 hr., Viking Fleet, ☏ **888/358-7477**).

🛏 $$$ **Atlantic Inn,** High St. (☏ **800/224-7422** or 401/466-5883; www.atlanticinn.com). $$ **Spring House Hotel,** 902 Spring St. (☏ **800/234-9263** or 401/466-5844; www.springhousehotel.com).

Sanibel Island
Seashells, Seashells, by the Seashore
Florida, U.S.A.

FOR YOUNG SEASHELL HUNTERS, THERE'S NO MORE REWARDING SPOT than down on the Gulf Coast of Florida, on a little apostrophe of coastal keys that lies attached by a long causeway to Fort Myers. Sanibel Island is a superb family beach destination for other reasons too—fine sugary white sand, healthy stands of palm trees, 22 miles (35km) of paved bike paths, limits on high-rises and tacky development, and the amount of land devoted to wildlife refuges. (Don't miss the Ding Darling Wildlife Refuge, a great place to kayak or hike on boardwalk paths through the mangrove swamps.) But it's the shell-hunting that the kids will remember, with some 200 species scattered openly on Sanibel's wide, placid beaches, no digging required. Bring a big pail, because you'll quickly fill it with whelks, olives, scallops, sand dollars, and conch—and maybe some rarer specimens too.

Sanibel has four public beach-access areas with metered parking: the eastern point around Sanibel Lighthouse, which has a fishing pier; Gulfside City Park, at the end of Algiers Lane, off Casa Ybel Road; Tarpon Bay Road Beach, at the south end of Tarpon Bay Road; and Bowman's Beach, off Sanibel-Captiva Road. Sanibel's prime season for shell hunting is February to April, or after any storm; low tide is the best time of day. Shells can be sharp, so wear Aqua Socks or old running shoes whenever you go walking on the beach. Just make sure to peer inside to check whether there are living creatures still inside—Florida law prohibits taking live shells from the beaches.

There's even a shell museum here: the **Bailey-Matthews Shell Museum,** 3075 Sanibel-Captiva Rd. (www.shellmuseum.org), devoted solely to saltwater, freshwater, and land shells. Shells from as far away as South Africa surround a 6-foot globe in the

Shell-seekers doing the Sanibel Stoop.

main exhibit hall, showing their geographic origins. Most fun is the Wheel of Fortune–shaped case identifying shells likely to wash up on Sanibel.

To find really rare shells, you can always head for the adjacent shoals and nearby small islands; **Captiva Cruises** (✆ **239/472-5300;** www.captivacruises.com) runs shelling trips, departing from the South Seas Resort on nearby Captiva Island, and several charter-boat skippers also will take guests on shelling expeditions (you can find several of them at the Sanibel Marina on North Yachtsman Drive, off Periwinkle Way east of Causeway Blvd.). You may have to bring an extra suitcase to tote all your treasures home.

ⓘ Information kiosk on Causeway Rd. ✆ **239/472-1080;** www. sanibel-captiva.org.

✈ Fort Myers International (19 miles/31km).

🛏 $ **Palm View Motel,** 706 Donax St. (✆ **877/472-1606** or 239/472-1606; www.palmviewsanibel.com). $$$ **Sundial Beach Resort,** 1451 Middle Gulf Dr. (✆ **866/565-5093;** www.sundial resort.com).

Santa Monica State Beach
California Classic

Santa Monica, California, U.S.A.

PICK YOUR SOUTHERN CALIFORNIA REFERENCE POINT—A BEACH BOYS album cover, a scene from Baywatch, or maybe (for the kids) episodes of Zoey 101. Wherever your image of classic Southern California beach comes from, Santa Monica fulfills it: 3.5 miles (5.6km) of wide golden-sand beach, with the Pacific Ocean sparkling blue-green beyond, and gently rolling white-fringed surf that the kids can jump in to their hearts' content.

Well-groomed Santa Monica State Beach is easy to get to as well, located right at the end of the Santa Monica Freeway and the starting point of the Pacific Coast Highway (PCH, otherwise known as California Highway 1). Colorado Boulevard leads directly to the Santa Monica pier; turn north on PCH or south along Ocean Avenue to find convenient parking. Four pedestrian bridges arch over the Pacific Coast Highway, connecting grassy Palisades Park to the beach. You can even bike, jog, or skate here on the paved beach path, which goes north as far as Malibu 66 and south to nearby funky Venice Beach 46 and beyond.

Even on a summer Sunday, this wide strand can be blissfully uncrowded, with well-maintained restrooms and a minimum of shoreline clutter. Surfing is limited to certain sections of the beach (check with lifeguards) and public beach volleyball courts are located south of the Pier. One focal point of the beach's recreational facilities is the Annenberg Beach House (415 Pacific Coast Hwy., ℂ 310/458-4904; admission charged), restored and adapted from a 1920s-era beachfront estate; among its amenities are a large swimming pool, a cafe, a fitness room, classes, and concessions for renting beach equipment.

At the southern end of the beach, you can also visit the vintage **Santa Monica Pier** (Ocean Avenue and Colorado Boulevard; ℂ 310/458-8901; www.santamonicapier.org), a relic of the area's 19th-century seaside resort days. Built in 1908 for passenger and cargo ships, the wooden wharf is now home to seafood restaurants

The Santa Monica Pier.

and snack bars; its landmark centerpiece is a gaily colored 1922 wooden carousel (which Paul Newman operated in the movie *The Sting*). The **Pier Aquarium,** by the carousel, displays local marine animals; halfway down the Pier, the **Pacific Park** amusement area (✆ **310/260-8744; www.pacpark.com**) has a Ferris wheel, roller coaster, and other rides. Anglers find some surprisingly good fishing from the pier's end.

The fulcrum of a 60-mile (97km) beachfront stretching along Santa Monica Bay from Malibu to the Palos Verde Peninsula, Santa Monica is prime real estate, with stylish oceanfront hotels and an artsy atmosphere. Before or after a beach outing, stroll a few blocks inland to the **Third Street Promenade,** a pedestrian-only outdoor mall. After all, mall shopping—that's another iconic Southern California activity.

ⓘ www.santamonica.com.

✈ Los Angeles International.

🛏 $$ **Cal Mar Hotel Suites,** 22 California Ave., Santa Monica (✆ **800/776-6007** or 310/395-5555; www.calmarhotel.com). $ **Sea Shore Motel,** 2637 Main St., Santa Monica (✆ **310/392-2787;** www.seashoremotel.com).

Poipu Beach
Lizard Legends & Shave Ice
Kauai, Hawaii, U.S.A.

Ask your kids to picture a tropical wilderness—it'll probably look just like Kauai. No surprise, because that image was planted in their minds by movies like *King Kong, Raiders of the Lost Ark,* and *Jurassic Park,* all of which were filmed here on the Garden Isle.

With its mossy rainforests, sparkling waterfalls, and limited resort development, easygoing Kauai is the island where Hawaiians themselves go for a relaxing getaway. Having already escaped the crowds by coming to Kauai, you don't really have to worry about escaping the "crowds" of Poipu, the popular resort area on Kauai's south coast. If anything, your challenge is to decide which of Poipu's beaches best suits your family.

Right at the center of things, large **Poipu Beach Park** is actually two beaches in one. Head to the left of the sandbar and you find a

Spouting Horn.

gentle, child-friendly sandy-bottom pool protected by a lava-rock jetty. Head to the right and you face an open bay of vivid turquoise water that attracts swimmers, snorkelers, surfers, and boogie-boarders, a perfect place for would-be surfers to ride their first waves. Facilities include a lifeguard, restrooms, showers, and free parking in the red-dirt lot. Behind the beach, a grassy lawn lined with coconut palms makes a great place to enjoy a sand-free pic-nic, or perhaps indulge in a traditional Hawaiian shave ice cone from **Brennecke's Beach Broiler.** (Brennecke's is such a local landmark, many people refer to the eastern half of Poipu Beach as Brennecke's Beach.)

For a more adventurous outing, head east past the Grand Hyatt Kauai on a red-dirt road to unspoiled **Mahaulepu Beach,** 2 miles (3km) of reddish-gold sand at the foot of Haupu Ridge. Mahaulepu is ideal for beachcombing and shell hunting—check out the beach rock to find a Hawaiian petroglyph of a voyaging canoe. There's no lifeguard, however, and swimming can be risky, though you can safely wade into the reef-sheltered shallows just west of the parking lot.

Another day, head west on Lawai Beach Road. Turn off at Hoona Road to find a tiny golden-sand cove known as **Baby Beach,** where the placid protected waters are wonderful for toddlers. (**Note:** When the tide is high, the beach may nearly disappear.) Just west of Baby Beach, the narrow sands of **Lawai Beach** offer beginning snorkelers relatively calm waters. Continue west a few minutes to **Spouting Horn Park**—there's no beach here, but a famous blow hole in the coastal shelf spouts water and makes an eerie roar at high tide. Legend says it's a giant lizard trapped in the rocks—even if the kids don't buy that story, they'll love the rainbow shimmer of the shooting water at sunset.

ⓘ www.poipu-beach.org.

✈ Lihue, Kauai.

🛏 $$ **Outrigger Kiahuna Plantation,** 2253 Poipu Rd., Koloa (ⓒ **866/956-4262** or 808/742-6411; www.outrigger.com). $$ **Nihi Kai Villas,** 1870 Ho'one Rd., Poipu Beach (ⓒ **800/325-5701** or 808/742-2000; www.parrishkauai.com).

Rügen
Baltic Beach Party
Germany

GERMANY DOESN'T HAVE MUCH SEACOAST, AND MOST OF IT'S ON THE Baltic Sea—hardly renowned for sun and fun. Yet the resort island of Rügen will surprise you with its alabaster beaches and copious sunshine. Rügen gets 100 more hours of annual sunshine than Munich does, making it plenty warm in summer for all sorts of watersports. Strong Baltic breezes encourage windsurfing, kite-surfing, waveboarding, and water skiing, and because it's so far north, daylight lingers for hours, extending your beach day well past supper time.

Separated by a narrow strait from Germany's northeast coast, Rügen Island is Germany's largest island—more like a chunk of land severed from the mainland, with a varied landscape of stark white chalk cliffs, tranquil wetlands, fairy-tale beech forests, and sand fringed bays. Once the Prussians took over this area—formerly Pomerania—from Sweden in 1815, seaside spas began to be built on Rügen; by the 1870s elegant Rügen holidays were the height of fashion. In the 1930s, the Nazis began to build a mega-resort at Prora, but World War II interrupted; after the war, Rügen's East German rulers built utilitarian holiday centers here to reward union stalwarts with cheap holidays—a sad come-down from Rügen's glory days.

Since reunification, however, those holiday centers have been rejuvenated as lively resorts, with extensive recreational facilities—families will find non-stop activities, everything from crazy golf to pirate games to trampolines. Not only that, the island offers a hand-ful of charmingly old-school theme parks—such as the **Rugenpark** miniature village in Gingst, **Dinosaurierland** in Spyker, and the low-key roller coasters of **Inselrodelbahn Bergen** in Bergen—plus the narrow gauge **Rasender Roland** (www.rasender-roland.com) steam train that putters along the east coast, connecting the resort towns of Putbus, Sellin, Baabe, and Göhren. It's not quite Myrtle Beach **35**, but you won't run out of things to do.

The best swimming beaches tend to be on the east coast, facing the open Baltic—the long sandy stretch known as the **Schaabe** (various sections are known as Drewoldke, Glowe and Breege) and to the south, the sprawling **Ostseebad** curving from Sassnitz to Göhren. The strands at **Prora** and **Binz** are the longest Ostseebad beaches, with fine sand and gentle surf that make them ideal for small children. Surfers gravitate to the northern beaches of **Drankse** and **Wiek** and the headlands at **Sassnitz.**

In those long mellow Baltic summer evenings, you can stroll along Binz's historic wooden promenade, past beautifully preserved 19th-century villas, and almost imagine you've stepped back in time—never mind the weight in your arms of a sleeping, sand-covered kid who begged to stay at the beach "just a little longer, pleeeease!"

ⓘ www.ruegen.de or www.ostseebad-binz.de.

✈ Berlin (317km/197 miles).

🛏 $$ **Aquamaris,** Wittower Strasse 4, Seebad, Juliusruh (ⓒ **49/38391/444 05;** www.aquamaris.de). $$ **IFA Rügen Hotel & Ferienpark,** Strandpromenade 74, Ostseebad Binz (ⓒ **49/ 38393/91102;** www.lopesan.com).

Bring the Family

Cambrils
Break from Barcelona
Costa Dorada, Spain

BEAUTIFUL BARCELONA, FAMED FOR ITS SUPERB FOOD, ARCHITECTURE, shopping, and nightlife—you'll surely want to include it on your family's Spanish vacation itinerary. But when the museums and tapas bars begin to wear thin, scoop the kids up and head down the N-340 highway, tracing the pine-covered headlands and over-looking mountains of the Mediterranean coast. Your destination, only an hour south of Barcelona: the wide, gently shelving golden sands of Cambrils. You'll need no better proof that this region of Catalonia deserves its nickname, Costa Dorada—aka Golden Coast.

A wave of resort development in the 1960s brought high-rise hotels to many of Cambrils' neighboring towns, but Cambrils still wears the character of a traditional Spanish fishing village, with narrow cobbled streets, crumbling medieval walls, an atmospheric market hall, and an enclosed harbor with a bright-red lighthouse. More recently, the Catalonian government has certified it as a Des-tinació de Turisme Familiar (Family Tourism Destination), which means that buildings conform to certain safety codes and family-friendly activities predominate.

South of the fishing port, a series of breakwaters create some 9km (5½ miles) of scalloped golden-sand beaches. This is highly civilized beachgoing: Resort hotels line the seafront, and every beach provides lifeguards, showers, food stands, and beach gear concessions (pedal boats are very popular around here). Their gentle slopes provide lots of calm shallows where toddlers and babies can safely dabble in the water. **La Llosa** and **L'Ardiaca,** the closest to town, are usually not too crowded; the next beach out, **L'Horta de Santa Maria,** is extremely popular, its sands and water so clean that it has earned a Blue Flag certification. The sand's a little rockier at busy **La Riera;** surfers add to the crowds at **Prat de'N Forés/ Regueral,** another Blue Flag beach. There's a kids club at Regueral, and another at neighboring **Del Cavet,** which is a little quieter but has coarser sand. As you continue away from town, more beachgoers flock to the lovely Blue Flag beaches of **l'Esquirol, Vilafortuny,** and **Cap de Sant Pere.**

Many European families plop down here for an entire week or longer, reveling in the Costa Dorada's buoyant blue waters and easygoing lifestyle. Even with those gorgeous beaches only steps away, many of the oceanfront hotels have swimming pools too—you can't have too much of a good thing!—as well as play-rooms and children's programs. But if you need any more persuad-ing, get this: Only 13km (9 miles) away lies one of Spain's most popular amusement parks, **Port Aventura** (www.portaventura.cat).

Different section of the park have rides and restaurants themed to various regions of the world—the Mediterranean, Polynesia, China, the Wild West, and (why not?) Sesame Street.

ⓘ www.cambrils-tourism.com.

✈ Barcelona (109km/68 miles).

🛏 $ **Hotel Vila Mar,** Pais Basc 10, Cambrils (© **34/977/381154;** www.augustushotels.es). $$$ **Tryp Port Cambrils Sol Melià,** Rambla Regueral 11, Cambrils (© **888/956-3542** or 34/977/358 600; www.solmelia.com).

28 Bring the Family

Whitehaven Beach
Wonder Down Under
Queensland, Australia

THE KIDS WILL PROBABLY RECOGNIZE WHITEHAVEN BEACH INSTANTLY— it's the most-photographed beach in Australia, its image plastered all over postcards and travel posters and brochures. Ah, so *this* is what the Great Barrier Reef is supposed to look like.

Whitehaven Beach is the star attraction on Whitsunday Island, the largest of 74 islands in the Whitsunday archipelago, midway between the Queensland coast and the outer Great Barrier Reef. Island-hopping around the Whitsundays is many Australians' idea of a perfect holiday, whether by chartered sailboat or on a multi-island cruise. Only 8 of the Whitsundays are inhabited—"inhabited" meaning there's a single resort, surrounded by protected parkland. (The one Whitsunday with extensive services is Hamilton Island.) With fringing reefs around every island, the swimming and snorkeling is generally fantastic, although most islands have only rocky coral coves, which makes Whitehaven Beach all the more striking.

Whitehaven Beach.

Big as it is, Whitsunday Island has no resort—it's all national parkland, covered with dense pine and eucalyptus forest (no swaying tropical palm trees here). That dense green tangle only accentuates the sugary white sand of aptly-named Whitehaven Beach, on the island's southeastern tip. Whitehaven is truly breathtaking, a swoop of sand 7km (4 miles) long and so dazzling white, it almost hurts your eyes. It's a freak of nature, its fine silica sand deposited here by prevailing currents from the mainland (there is no silica in the island's native rocks). That fine sand also underlies the crystal-clear aquamarine shallows of Hill Inlet, and as tides sweep the sea floor's sands, colors shift and swirl dramatically over the inlet (the effect is especially stunning at low tide). Hike up to the lookout at Tongue Point, at Hill Inlet's north end, for panoramic views.

In 2010 CNN named Whitehaven Beach the world's best eco-friendly beach; its protected status in this national park keeps it pristine and unspoiled. (All visitors must register with the park.) Nevertheless, it's so famous that plenty of day-trippers come every day on tour boats. Sightseeing flights over the island deliver that dazzling aerial view without really getting up close—without dipping into those warm aquamarine waters and feeling your own feet sift through that powdery sand.

There are several park campgrounds, however, if you want to rough it and stay overnight. It's a great way to experience the beauty of the Great Barrier Reef for kids who may not yet be ready for serious snorkeling and/or diving. You simply can't come to the Whitsundays and miss Whitehaven Beach—and no matter how many pictures the kids have seen, in person it's even more amazingly beautiful.

ⓘ www.whitsundaytourism.com.

✈ Great Barrier Reef Airport, Hamilton Island.

🚢 **Cruise Whitsundays** (www.cruisewhitsundays.com) and **Fantasea Adventure Cruising** (www.fantasea.com.au).

🛏 $$ **Palm Bungalows,** Hamilton Island (✆ **866/209-0891** or 61/2/9433 0444; www.hamiltonisland.com.au). $$ **Water's Edge Resort,** Airlie Beach (✆ **61/7/4948 2655;** www.watersedge whitsundays.com.au).

29 **Bring the Family**

Antigua
A Beach a Day
Leeward Islands, The Caribbean

ONCE, THE BRITISH COLONY OF ANTIGUA WAS KNOWN FOR ITS SUGAR plantations; today this independent nation is known for a different kind of sugar—the fine white sand of its myriad beaches. It may sound like a tourist office gimmick, but it's pretty much true: Antigua has a beach for every day of the year. Okay, so maybe there are only 364 beaches, but that's still pretty amazing for an island of this size. And when you consider what quality beaches they are— all of them open to the public—well, it's pretty safe to award Antigua with the crown of Best Beach Island in the Caribbean.

Lodging on Antigua tends to be in small-scale luxury resorts, each with its own splendid chunk of beachfront real estate. But kids can get bored with the same experience day after day, so Antigua's wealth of beach options becomes a real advantage. Note that the west coast, which faces the Caribbean, has more tranquil waters, while the east coast's Atlantic-facing shores have more wind and wave action.

The gentle turquoise waves and powdery white sand of **Dickenson Bay,** on the northwest coast, are popular with families (handy concessions are also a plus); nearby Paradise Reef offers good snorkeling. **Johnson's Point,** on Antigua's southwestern tip, offers more solitude, but the trade-off is no facilities; snorkelers, however, appreciate the bonanza of rainbow-hued tropical fish in its clear, tranquil waters. Near Johnson's Point, idyllic **Turner's Beach** invites beach lounging with a stretch of fine white sand. As you move north of here, closer to the Jolly Harbour marina, the beaches get progressively more populated, especially when cruise ships are in port, as visitors gravitate to lovely **Driftwood Beach** and the shimmering blue waters of **Darkwood Beach.**

Antigua.

On the southern coast, kids may be interested to see the point where the calm Caribbean meets the more turbulent Atlantic below the bluffs of **Carlisle Bay.** If you're taking them sightseeing at the historic British naval port at English Harbour, make it a day with a beach stop at lovely white-sand **Pigeon Point** at Falmouth Harbour. On the southeastern coast, the kicked-up Atlantic surf at beautiful **Half-Moon Bay** is a windsurfer haven; north of here, **Long Bay's** shallow crystal-blue waters offer stunning coral reefs and **Pineapple Beach** lures beach buffs with nearly perfect white sands.

Kitschy as it is, *Pirates of the Caribbean* fans may not be able to resist another Antiguan feature: a day sail with **Pirates of Antigua** (© **268/562-7946;** www.piratesofantigua.com), a jaunty motorized replica of a pirate ship. Can you blame them for wanting to give that a spin?

ⓘ www.antigua-barbuda.org.

✈ V.C. Bird International Airport, Antigua.

🛏 $$$ **The Verandah Resort & Spa,** Indian Town Rd., Dian Bay (© **866/237-1785** or 268/562-6848; www.verandahresortand spa.com). $$ **Siboney Beach Club,** Dickenson Bay (© **800/533-0234** in the U.S. or 268/462-0806; www.caribbean-resort-antigua-hotel-siboney-beach.com).

30   Bring the Family

Coronado Island
Some Like It Hot
San Diego, California, U.S.A.

MAPS WILL TELL YOU THAT CORONADO ISN'T REALLY AN ISLAND; IT'S A peninsula, anchored to the mainland by a long strip of barrier beach called the Silver Strand. But San Diegans still refer to it as Coronado Island; it sure feels like an island, floating serenely on the other side of San Diego Bay from downtown San Diego. Dotted with palm trees, sailboats bobbing in its marina, cool breezes and gentle surf caressing its broad white Pacific beach—it seems a world apart.

You arrive via the majestic 2¼-mile (3.6km) swoop of the Coronado Bridge, arching high over the bay so that Navy ships can pass underneath. The views from the bridge are spectacular—you can even see Mexico in the distance. Eventually, at the far end of palm-lined Orange Avenue, the main street of Coronado's cozy "downtown," Coronado's crowning glory comes into view: the **Hotel Del Coronado,** aka the Hotel Del. Even if you've never seen the classic comedy *Some Like It Hot,* which was shot here in 1959, you'll instantly recognize there's something special about this landmark hotel, with its white Victorian turrets, red roof, and long oceanview veranda. It's the quintessential seaside villa, writ large. (In the movie, the resort is supposed to be in Florida, but never mind.) It's said that Coronado resident L. Frank Baum based the Emerald City in *The Wizard of Oz* on the Hotel Del, and it's certainly feels magical enough for that to be true.

Not only is the Del a marvelous hotel, it's located on a spectacular boulder-lined golden beach—a family-friendly municipal beach that anybody can enjoy. The hotel is on the main section, known as **Central Beach,** which tends to attract the most swimmers. (In the film, Tony Curtis woos Marilyn Monroe on this beach by chatting about seashell collecting.) There are several access points along Ocean Boulevard; finding a parking spot is the challenge. As you head north, the coastline curves toward the naval base, creating **North Beach,** where dogs are allowed and surfers ride a break known as the Outlet. South of the Del, The Shores follows Silver Strands Boulevard, lined with condo towers; the waves here are good for longboarding and boogie-boarding.

Staying at the Del isn't cheap, though it would be a splurge the kids would never forget. You don't have to be a hotel guest to eat in the Del's restaurants, shop in its boutiques, rent beach equipment, or rent bicycles (a good way to poke around town); across the road, you can rent boats or kayaks at the marina. If nothing else, find some excuse to stroll through its sumptuous, wood-paneled lobby and peek into its interior courtyard. It's the grand old lady of beach hotels, for sure.

ⓘ Tourist office, 1100 Orange Ave. (☎ **866/599-7242** or 619/437-8788; www.coronadovisitorcenter.com).

✈ San Diego (8 miles/13km).

🛏 $$$ **Hotel Del Coronado,** 1500 Orange Ave. (☎ **800/468-3533** or 619/435-6611; www.hoteldel.com). $ **The Coronado Village Inn,** 1017 Park Place (☎ **619/435-9318;** www.coronado villageinn.com).

Bring the Family

31

Ocracoke Island
Old Salt
North Carolina, U.S.A.

IMAGINE THE DREAD PIRATE BLACKBEARD, AKA EDWARD TEACH, concealing his ship among the scrubby oaks of Ocracoke Island, waiting to take merchant ships by surprise. Teach's favorite cruising ground, "Teach's Hole," lay at the southern tip of the island, offshore from what is now Springer's Point Nature Preserve on Loop Road. There Teach finally met his end in 1718, killed in a skirmish with British naval ships.

You can get the whole colorful story at the museum/shop **Teach's Hole,** Highway 12 at West End Rd. (☎ **252/928-1718**). Pirate lore is irresistible to some kids, and they'll really feel its salty spirit as you chug across Pamlico Sound to Ocracoke Island. One of the most remote of the Outer Banks barrier islands, Ocracoke anchors the southern end of the Cape Hatteras National Seashore. There are no bridges to Ocracoke, only ferries, from either Cape Hatteras ㉑ or across the wide, shallow Pamlico Sound from the mainland. It's 15 miles (24km) long and less than 656 ft. (200m) wide in some places, strung together along sand-dusted two-lane Highway 12, running the length of the island. Yet along this long skinny barrier island lie some of the East Coast's most beautiful tawny beaches, most of them pristine and undeveloped.

Wide flat Ocracoke Beach consistently makes it onto Top Ten Beaches lists (in 2007 it won the nation's top honor from beach expert Dr. Stephen Leatherman, aka "Doctor Beach") It's definitely a beauty, edged with low dunes, with frothy white surf rolling up in near-perfect precision. Thanks to the Gulf Stream, the water here is warmer than in other Outer Banks sites; it's rarely crowded, and parking is conveniently close to the sand, all of which makes it great for younger swimmers. Though there are no concessions, there are restrooms and showers, and lifeguards are on duty all summer long. Like any Outer Banks beach, it has enough rip currents and strong waves to require caution. And don't miss the nearby **Pony Pens,** where rangers tend Ocracoke's native ponies, whose ancestors were wrecked here on 17th-century Spanish galleons.

An isolated outpost for centuries, Ocracoke Island still has only about 750 year-round residents, their distinctive dialect betraying Cockney traces of Elizabethan-era English settlers. The squat, whitewashed **Ocracoke Lighthouse,** built in 1823 at Ocracoke's southern point, is still a working lighthouse, the second-oldest in the country. Ocracoke Village, the island's only real town, looks weathered and historic. There are no chain hotels or fast-food franchises here, only tidy rental cottages and quaint B&Bs. Wooden cafes line Ocracoke Village's Silver Lake harborside—before you hop on the ferry home, shake the sand out of your shoes and stop for a bowl of briny Hatteras clam chowder.

ⓘ www.ocracokevillage.com. **Cape Hatteras Seashore National Park** (ⓒ **252/473-2111;** www.nps.gov/caha).

✈ Ocracoke.

⛴ 30 min. from Hatteras (free) or 2½ hr. from Cedar Island or Swan Quarter. www.ncdot.org/transit/ferry or ⓒ 800/BY-FERRY.

🛏 $$ **The Anchorage Inn and Marina,** 205 Highway 12, Ocracoke Island (ⓒ **252/928-1101;** www.theanchorageinn.com). $$ **The Ocracoke Harbor Inn,** 144 Silver Lake Rd., Ocracoke Island (ⓒ **888/456-1998** or 252/928-5731; www.ocracokeharborinn.com).

The Ocracoke lighthouse, built in 1823, is the second oldest in the U.S.

Crane Beach
Happy as a Clam
Ipswich, Massachusetts, U.S.A.

CLAM LOVERS KNOW ALL ABOUT THE IPSWICH FLATS, A TIDAL STRETCH of the Atlantic just north of Boston where the fattest and tastiest clams hang out, waiting to be dug up and then deep-fried. Classic clam shacks along this part of the North Shore attract summertime crowds from all over the Boston area; a roadside Ipswich clam dinner is an annual ritual for many vacationers en route to the Maine coast or Lake Winnipesaukee.

North of the rocky drama of Cape Ann, where seafaring towns like Gloucester (as depicted in *A Perfect Storm*) seem pitted against the wild Atlantic, this last stretch of Massachusetts's Atlantic coast has a more modest wind-swept charm. Though the coastline is still predominantly rocky, and the water bracingly cold even in summer, there are a handful of delightful sandy dunescapes where locals chill out on long summer days. Prime among them is popular **Crane Beach,** off Argilla Road on the outskirts of the suburban town of Ipswich. Crane Beach is part of a 1,400-acre (567-hectare) reservation on the Castle Neck peninsula, originally part of the seaside estate of the wealthy Crane family. Today a boardwalk path leads over shifting dunes to this broad white sand beach sloping down to Ipswich Bay. It's an important nesting site for piping plovers (respect fenced-off areas April–July), and behind the beach a number of nature trails wind around the coastal dunes and the wetlands of the Essex River estuary.

Most summer visitors, however, are area families drawn to Crane's calmer surf and wide clean sands. Despite a fairly stiff admission price (up to $25 if you don't have a member's parking sticker), Crane Beach gets a lot of traffic during the short New England beach season. There may not be much room between your towel and your neighbor's, but it's a well-behaved and easygoing crowd. In season, the beach has lifeguards, restrooms, showers, picnic tables, and a simple snack bar. The parking lot fills up early—if you don't plan to spend the whole day here, try coming after 3pm, when admission is discounted and some cars have already left. To alleviate the parking crunch, on summer weekends **Ipswich Essex Explorer** buses (www.ipswich-essexexplorer.com) shuttle out to the beach from the Ipswich train station. Note: August is mosquito and green-fly season—bring insect repellent.

After you've left the beach, of course, local custom demands that you head back into Ipswich to stop at the **Clam Box** (246 High St., Ipswich, ✆ **978/356-9707**; www.ipswichma.com/clambox) for some fried clams. (The shack is hard to miss—it looks exactly like a giant gray clapboard box with the flaps folded open at the top.) Ah, that's the taste of a New England summer.

✈ Boston Logan International (29 miles/47km).

🛏 $$ **Atlantis Oceanfront Motor Inn,** 125 Atlantic Rd., Gloucester (✆ **800/732-6313** or 978/283-0014, www.atlantis motorinn.com). $$ **Arbor Inn Motel,** 153 High St., Ipswich, (✆ **978/356-0220,** www.arborinnmotel.com).

33 Bring the Family

Siesta Beach
And the Winner Is . . .
Siesta Key, Florida, U.S.A.

FOR YEARS, SIESTA BEACH WAS ALWAYS IN THE RUNNING, CROPPING up on various "best beach" lists. In 1987, it even won the Great International White Sand Beach Challenge. But finally, in 2011, Dr. Stephen Leatherman—aka "Doctor Beach"—gave Siesta Beach the #1 spot on his definitive America's Best Beaches list. His criteria? Siesta's clean, dazzling white sand and the purity of its azure waters. He also gave a shout-out to Siesta Beach's mild foam-edged surf and its gradual slope into the Gulf of Mexico—features that make Siesta Beach pretty much ideal for families.

Unlike Longboat Key to the north, the long barrier island of Siesta Key closely hugs Florida's west coast, only a marina's width away from the Sarasota-to-Venice coastline, conveniently attached by two causeways across Roberts Bay and Little Sarasota Bay. Retiree-magnet Sarasota already boasts a tony cultural calendar, but across the causeway residential Siesta Key is even more artsy, with a community of artisans and writers year-round. Forward-thinking Siesta Key residents long ago ensured that this 40-acre (16-hectare) swath of white sand, between Siesta Village and Point o' Rocks, would forever be kept open to the public, not snapped up by hotel developers as so much of the coast has been. More recently, regulations were also passed to make it a smoke-free zone—more good news for families with young kids.

The one thing you can't forget once you've been to Siesta Beach is how white its sand is, even compared to other Southwest Florida strands. Stretching hundreds of yards wide, that fine sand is composed of almost 99% quartz, instead crushed shells. It fairly sparkles in the Florida sunshine, and it doesn't retain heat—it won't burn the soles of your children's bare feet on a blazing summer day.

Siesta Beach has all the expected public amenities: restrooms, showers, a snack bar, a picnic area, a few welcome shade trees, and a 700-car parking lot—though big as it is, it fills up on weekends. When Siesta gets crowded, it's good to know that you have a couple of other public alternatives in the area: white **Crescent Beach,** just south of Siesta Beach, and quiet **Turtle Beach** at Siesta Key's south end. There's also a strip of beach at Siesta Village, with its congenial clutter of casual restaurants and pubs along Ocean Boulevard. (If you've got teenagers with you, they may welcome a chance to hang out at night at Siesta Village's noisy music clubs.)

If you can, try to hit Siesta Beach an hour before sunset on Sunday evenings, when the weekly Sunday drum circle gathers by Siesta Beach's main pavilion. It's a great community gathering, fun and just a little eccentric.

✈ Sarasota-Bradenton International.

🛏 $$ **Captiva Beach Resort,** 6772 Sara Sea Circle, Siesta Key (℃ **800/349-4131** or 941/349-4131; www.captivabeachresort. com). $$ **Tropical Breeze Resort,** 140 Columbus Blvd., Siesta Key (℃ **800/300-2492** or 941/349-1125; www.tropicalbreezeinn.com).

Bethany Beach
Listen to the Quiet
Delaware, U.S.A.

PULLING INTO THE HEART OF BETHANY BEACH, TRAFFIC PARTS ON either side of a red cedar totem pole—a carved portrait of Nanti-coke chief Little Owl, with an eagle on his head. Locals grumbled when it was first erected in 1976, saying it wasn't authentic. Now it's such a beloved landmark, they've replaced it three times.

Bethany Beach isn't fond of change, and that's one of its best qualities. Situated halfway between bustling Rehoboth Beach, Delaware, and Ocean City, Maryland, Bethany Beach has carved out a very different niche, with a laid-back atmosphere and family-friendly establishments. This Delaware beach town comes hon-estly by its nickname "The Quiet Resort." Originally founded in 1900 by the Disciples of Christ as a religious seaside retreat, it still tends to be socially conservative—slow to grant its first liquor license (not until 1982) yet quick to impose a town smoking ban (2011). While that might disappoint partying singles, it's great for families seeking a wholesome resort atmosphere, which is why Bethany Beach's vacation rentals book up earlier every year, usually with repeat visitors.

With neither a railroad nor a harbor, Bethany Beach was a charming backwater in the pre-automobile era. Things picked up after the Chesapeake Bay Bridge improved highway access in 1952, but even then, Bethany Beach was never rocked by a real-estate boom. Its only high-rises are the Sea Colony development, built south of town in 1969, which so shocked some Bethany Beachers that the experiment has never been repeated.

The 1-mile–long (1.6km) **Bethany Beach Boardwalk** is more of a breezy open promenade than a strip of concessions; instead of bars or dance clubs, local amusements are likely to feature mini-golf courses (with pirate or Viking themes) or go-carts. The town's lifeguarded public beach is often packed on summer afternoons, but it's easily accessed (most families walk from their rental houses); the surf is gentle, and the water's surprisingly warm from May through October.

The area's flat terrain also makes it easy to bicycle around. Directly north of town on coastal Highway 1 lies the unspoiled 6-mile-long (9.5km) barrier beach of Delaware Seashore State Park. The Seashore's **Indian River Marina** is a good place for kayaking; nature trails wind through its coastal dunes and wetlands. Head south on Highway 1 and you'll quickly reach the 3-mile-long (5km) barrier beach of **Fenwick Island State Park.** The kids will enjoy Fenwick's **DiscoverSea Shipwreck Museum** (708 Ocean Hwy.), and the park's **Little Assawoman Bay** is a great place for young-sters to try out windsurfing or sailing. Or show the kids how to dig up clams or go crabbing—perfect old-school summertime fun.

ⓘ www.bethany-fenwick.org.

✈ Ocean City (19 miles/31km).

🛏 $$$ **The Addy Sea Bed and Breakfast,** 99 Ocean View Pkwy., Bethany Beach (ⓒ **800/418-6764,** 302/539-3707; www.addysea.com). $$ **Bethany Arms Motel,** Atlantic Ave. and Holly-wood St., Bethany Beach (ⓒ **302/539-9603;** www.beach-net.com/bethanyarms.html).

Bring the Family　35

Myrtle Beach
Grandstand on the Grand Strand
South Carolina, U.S.A.

OFFICIALLY IT'S CALLED THE GRAND STRAND—A SWATH OF SOUTH Carolina coast that runs all the way from Little River to George-town. But most everyone refers to it as Myrtle Beach, after the perennially popular beach resort at the heart of the Grand Strand.

Back in colonial times, this area was practically deserted because its soil was too sandy to grow tobacco or cotton; today that sand is the region's greatest asset, offering some 60 miles (97km) of Atlantic beach. That hard-packed sand looks remarkably like brown sugar—a resemblance that many a toddler has tested over the years. For vacationing families, Myrtle Beach is shorthand for an all-in-one sun-plus-fun destination.

Nearly 15 million visitors come annually to the Myrtle Beach area, a number that has been growing steadily since the 1980s and shows no sign of stopping. High-rise hotels and condos line the lifeguarded public beach of Myrtle Beach proper, but elsewhere the beachfront skyline has been thoughtfully broken up, alternating landscaped residential zones with commercial zones. This downtown stretch has plenty of buzz, with lots of theme restaurants and shopping centers; a spiffy new 1¼-mile (2km) boardwalk and promenade opened in 2010, anchored by the brightly lit 18-story-high SkyWheel observation wheel, which offers sweeping ocean views. If you'd prefer a little more nature with your beach time, you can always escape to **Myrtle Beach State Park,** south of downtown, which provides more than 300 acres (121 hectares) of piney woods and access to a sandy beach; or explore the back bays of **Murrells Inlet** by kayak.

For many families, an annual pilgrimage to Myrtle Beach is a rite of summer, offering not just beach time but tons of kid-friendly amusements. The classic is waterfront **Family Kingdom** (300 S. Ocean Blvd.) amusement park, which has the state's largest Ferris wheel, but the boom of the past few years has added the state-of-the art **Ripley's Aquarium** (1110 Celebrity Circle); **Hard Rock Park** (211 George Bishop Pkwy.), with its hip yet family-friendly vibe; **Myrtle Waves Waterpark** (U.S. 17 Bypass at 10th Avenue N.), the state's largest water park; the automotive-themed **NASCAR Race Park** (U.S. 17 Bypass at 21st Avenue N.), and a clutch of other water parks, mini-golf courses, and kid-oriented themed entertainments. Golf has become a huge draw here, with nearly 250 courses in the area. Add to that all the usual watersports—sailing, parasailing, kayaking, surfing, windsurfing, fishing, catamarans, and banana boats, even scuba diving—and you'll have only yourself to blame if the kids get bored.

ⓘ www.visitmyrtlebeach.com.

✈ Myrtle Beach International Airport.

🛏 $$ **Resort Quest Myrtle Beach at the Market Common,** 1232 Farrow Parkway, Myrtle Beach (ⓒ **877/869-5962** or 843/238-1614; www.resortquestmyrtlebeach.com). $ **Coral Beach Resort & Suites,** 1105 S. Ocean Blvd., Myrtle Beach (ⓒ **800/556-1754** or 843/448-8421; www.thecoralbeach.com).

Bring the Family 36

Cannon Beach
Stacks of Fun
Oregon, U.S.A.

YOU CAN'T MISS THAT ROCK: HEAVING UP 235 FEET (7M) ABOVE THE cold Pacific waters at low tide, right by the shoreline, **Haystack Rock** is one of the Northwest Coast's most photogenic sights. Just imagine the explorer William Clark (of Lewis and Clark fame) marveling at it as he arrived here in 1806 to parley with some local Tillamook Indians over a beached whale.

Actually, Haystack Rock is a pretty prosaic name for this brooding, algae-draped basalt hulk; it's shaped more like a conquistador's helmet, or the nose of a lost spaceship (with those two side rocks, the Needles, for wing fins). You could mull this question over for hours as you laze away a summer afternoon on Cannon Beach, watching the rock's shadows lengthen in the slowly setting summer sun.

Meanwhile your kids will probably be busy investigating the other pleasures of this long tawny strand—kite-flying, boogie-boarding, kayaking, tidepooling, hunting for shells, or watching the adorable tufted puffins perched on the offshore rocks. Other options include a guided horseback ride along the beach (contact **Sea Ranch Stables,** www.cannon-beach.net/searanch) or pedaling a low-slung three-wheeled funcycle down the packed sands at

Haystack Rock.

low tide (contact **Mike's Bike Shop;** www.mikesbike.com). The waters can be cold and the winds stiff (hence the kite-flying), so the kids may prefer beachcombing to actual swimming—at least consider having them wear wet suits. The waters directly around Haystack Rock are a protected marine sanctuary, but there's plenty of other sea to frolic in.

Haystack Rock sits towards the northern end of 8-mile-long (13km) Cannon Beach, just south of the town of the same name. Many streets in town lead directly to the beach, with short beach access stairways cut into the low green bluffs. Once a renowned artists' community, Cannon Beach has now been discovered by the spa-and-B&B crowd, with upscale boutiques and galleries invading its weathered cedar-shingle buildings, picket fences, and quiet gravel lanes.

To escape the artsy browsers in high summer season, head up the coast a couple miles to the spruce forests of **Ecola State Park** (www.oregon.gov/oprd/parks). Inside the park, you can hike from Ecola Point to secluded **Crescent Beach,** or park at **Indian Beach** to watch the surfers and poke around its rich tidepools. A short steep hike up the bluffs from the Indian Beach parking lot brings you to a breathtaking view of Cannon Beach, Haystack Rock, and the **Tillamook Rock Lighthouse.** If Lewis and Clark had only brought their cameras with them . . .

ⓘ www.cannonbeach.org.

✈ Portland (79 miles/126km).

🛏 $$$ **Surfsand Resort,** 148 W. Gower St., Cannon Beach (ⓒ **800/547-6100** or 503/436-2274; www.surfsand.com). $$ **Hallmark Resort,** 1400 S. Hemlock St., Cannon Beach (ⓒ **888/448-4449** or 503/436-1566; www.hallmarkinns.com).

Sandown
The Wight Stuff
Isle of Wight, U.K.

In 1845, thanks to the arrival of two young lovebirds—Queen Victoria and Prince Albert—summering on this sun-kissed Channel Island became all the rage. Following the royal couple, a crush of 19th-century celebrities, from Alfred Lord Tennyson to Charles Dickens, simply had to vacation on the Isle of Wight. By the turn of the 19th century, 10 pleasure piers dotted the island, along with the U.K.'s oldest theme park, **Blackgang Chine,** opened in 1843.

But you don't need to tell the kids all that. Just tell them about the Isle of Wight's sandy beaches and sunny climate Sandown holds Britain's record for most days of sunshine per year, and feels almost Mediterranean compared to most of the U.K.

While the yachting crowd gravitates to Cowes (site of the first America's Cup race in 1851), families head for the twin towns of **Sandown** and **Shanklin** on the Isle of Wight's east coast. Set on lovely Sandown Bay, Sandown and Shanklin share a 9.7km-long (6-mile) sweep of groomed golden beach with a view of white chalk cliffs in the background. All three beaches on the bay have won Blue Flag status for their clean sands and clear waters; their gradual slope makes great safe swimming for young children. Sandown has vintage charm, with its 19th-century amusement pier stretching out over the water and a well-preserved Victorian-era esplanade along the sea wall. Shanklin has two cliff-sheltered beaches—**Small Hope Beach** to the north (which connects to Sandown Beach) and the main **Hope Beach,** with its own paved esplanade and amusement arcades. Kids get a kick out of riding the **Cliff Lift** from Shanklin beach to the town proper.

A water ride at Blackgang Chine, the U.K.'s oldest theme park.

A wide range of amusements are available off the seafront as well. At the interactive **Dinosaur Isle museum** (Culver Parade, Sandown), you'll learn that the Isle of Wight is one of Europe's most important fossil sites; the **Isle of Wight Zoo** (Yaverland Rd., Sandown), is known for its award-winning Tiger Sanctuary; and a short distance inland, exotic animals prowl naturalistic habitats at **Amazon World** (Watery Lane, Newchurch). Down the coast at Ventnor, **Blackgang Chine** (www.blackgangchine.com) still operates many of its original old-fashioned attractions (a hedge maze, water gardens, hall of mirrors) as well as more modern roller coasters and waterslides. Your family may also enjoy a ride on the restored **Isle of Wight Steam Railway** (www.iwsteamrailway.co.uk). Spend an afternoon hiking along dramatic chalk cliffs on sections of the panoramic Coastal Path, or climb up the picturesque wooded gorge of Shanklin Chine to rustic **Old Village** with its thatched-roof cottages. It's the sort of only-in-England experience you'll remember for years to come.

ⓘ www.iwight.com or www.islandbreaks.co.uk.

✈ London Heathrow (145km/90 miles).

🚢 Ryde (20 min. from Portsmouth), West Cowes (22 min. from Southampton), East Cowes (55 min. car ferry from Southampton).

🛏 $ **Malton House Hotel,** 8 Park Rd., Shanklin (ⓒ **44/1983/865007;** www.maltonhouse.co.uk). $$ **The Ocean Hotel,** Esplanade, Sandown (ⓒ **44/1983/402 351;** www.ocean-hotel.co.uk).

Local Color

38

Lamu
Swahili Sans Safari
Kenya

LYING OFF THE MOMBASA COAST JUST TWO DEGREES SOUTH OF THE equator, Lamu delivers a one-two punch—it looks like an exotic stage set, but it also happens to have amazing beaches. This long-forgotten medieval spice-trade outpost was barely changed by a hippie influx in the 1960s; even the creeping gentrification of recent years hasn't altered the island's dusty charm. There are only a couple of cars on the whole island, with donkeys providing all necessary transportation, squeezing past each other on often shoulder-width streets.

Visitors fly into **Lamu Town,** Kenya's oldest settlement and a listed World Heritage site. Because of its roots as a 14th-century Arab trading port, Lamu is largely Muslim, with a sprinkling of modest mosques and minarets; adding to the cultural mix, Portuguese cannons line the 19th-century waterfront, fronted with a "skyline" of distinctly Swahili thatched roofs. The women wear black veils, the older men long loose-flowing *djellabas*; shops and cafes shut up in the heat of the day. To escape the dazzling equatorial sun, you plunge into a labyrinth of arches and narrow lanes, lined with lime-washed stone houses, their Persian-flavored doorways flaunting intricate carved teak and mahogany. (Visit the Swahili House Museum near Juma Mosque for an inside glimpse of these traditional houses—the cool courtyards with their pools of mosquito-eating fish, the breeze-catching shaded verandas on the roof, the coral powder whitewash that insulates against the heat.)

After getting a taste of Lamu Town's unique cultural mosaic, most visitors then repair down the coast to the island's second town, **Shela.** A string of guesthouses cluster at one end of Shela's gorgeous golden sandy beach, which runs for 12km (7 miles) along the Indian Ocean, backed by ancient sand dunes. Swimming is ideal along this unspoiled stretch of open sand, with its gentle surf. Yet idyllic as it looks, some of the most famous families in the world have holiday homes here, installing surprisingly sleek décor inside Shela's medina-style townhouses. The island's African cuisine is inflected with haute European culinary trends, as you'll discover when you stop for a drink with the in crowd at the colonnaded Peponi Hotel.

Kenya's south coast is known for its spectacular coral reefs, with several underwater parks that attract divers in the know. Even further north, where Lamu is located, dolphins swim in the waters off shore; you'll probably meet a few when you're out for a dip. Better yet, devote one day of your stay to hire a traditional wooden *dhow*, or sailing boat, to explore the waters around the island, admiring its rich marine life of dugongs, turtles, and dolphins. Exotic on shore and off—that's the lure of Lamu.

ⓘ www.magicalkenya.com.

✈ Lamu airport (connect through Nairobi).

🛏 $$ **Stone House Hotel,** Lamu Old Town (℃ **254/42/4633-544;** www.stonehousehotellamu.com). $$$ **Peponi Hotel,** Shela Beach (℃ **254/20/802-3655;** www.peponi-lamu.com).

Hanalei Beach
The Garden Isle's Magic Bay
Kauai, Hawaii, U.S.A.

HALF THE FUN IS GETTING THERE. CRUISING ALONG THE TWO-LANE Kuhio Highway (Hwy. 56), which circles up the coast from Lihue, you begin to understand why Kauai is called the Garden Isle. The entire island is deliberately kept undeveloped—no high-rises or megaresorts, by law nothing taller than a coconut tree—but on the North Coast, the island's misty tropical beauty really reveals itself.

A spectacular sunset as seen from Hanalei Bay.

As you head west from Kilauea, for the next 5 or 6 miles (8 or 10km) things become steadily more rural—roadside fruit stands, grazing cattle, plunging waterfalls, and stiltlike bridges (don't miss the sweeping view at the Hanalei Valley Lookout). Just past the low-rise luxury resorts of Princeville, the road—now Hwy. 560—doubles around with a hairpin turn, depositing you down at the landmark Hanalei Bridge, a rusty one-lane steel truss bridge built in 1912. Another half-dozen one-lane bridges must be crossed before you reach the highway's end at Haena—clearly they aren't expecting traffic jams.

With its sleepy end-of-the-road vibe, Hanalei Town has just enough shops and restaurants lining the main road (there isn't much else to the town) for an afternoon's diversion. Cupped in a ring of green mountains, the coastal town's low-roofed wooden buildings offer a glimpse into Hawaii's 19th-century mission-era past, with landmarks like the green-frame **Waioli Huia Church** and its accompanying **Mission House museum.** A relic of Kauai's often-forgotten agricultural history, the historic Ho'opulapula Hariguchi Rice Mill in the **Hanalei National Wildlife Refuge** (Ohiki Road) is now a agrarian museum, set amid working taro fields.

Beguiling as the drive may be, however, most visitors to Hanalei come here to enjoy Hanalei Beach, an enchanting 2-mile-long (3km) half-moon of pale gold sand on the shores of Hanalei. (Yes, just like in the old folk song "Puff the Magic Dragon.") The name means "lei-shaped bay"—what could be more Hawaiian than that? Surfers congregate here in winter, but in summer, Hanalei Bay becomes as placid as a lake. The waves are gentle, the water aquamarine, the ocean bottom sandy and gently sloping; a backdrop of green-velvet Bali-Hai-style peaks rises in the distance, completing the image of paradise.

An ancient sunken valley, Hanalei Bay is a superb site for all sorts of water sports—bodyboarding, surfing, fishing, windsurfing, canoe paddling, kayaking, and boating. Three parks offer public access to the beach: **Hanalei Beach Pavilion Park, Waioli Beach Park,** and **Black Pot Park,** where you'll find a boat ramp and a picturesque long concrete pier, which ends in a roofed pavilion. With coral reefs on either side, a patch of coral in the middle, and a sunken ship to explore, it's a fun diving destination as well. You may not encounter any dragons, but it'll be magical nonetheless.

(i) www.kauaidiscovery.com. Hanalei Beach Park, Weke Rd., Kauai.

✈ Lihue (31 miles/50km)

🛏 $$$ **Hanalei Bay Resort,** 5380 Honoiki Rd., Princeville (✆ **407/996-3000** or 808/826-6522; www.hanaleibayresort.com). $$ **Hanalei Colony Resort,** 5-7130 Kuhio Hwy., Haena (✆ **800/628-3004** or 808/826-6235; www.hcr.com).

Placencia
Catching the Breeze in Belize
Belize

NESTLED IN THE CROOK OF CENTRAL AMERICA'S BEND LIES ONE OF THE world's most splendid coral reefs: The Belize Barrier Reef. Named a UNESCO World Heritage Site in 1996, it's the longest continuous barrier reef in the Northern Hemisphere, 306km (190 miles) of diverse marine habitat with superb water clarity and visibility. It's no surprise Belize should be one of the world's most popular diving destinations.

The hub of diving action has long been **Ambergris Caye,** Belize's largest offshore island. The only drawback to an Ambergris Caye vacation: It has few long beaches, and the shore waters are full of seagrass, a key ingredient for coral reef health. Most swimmers dive off of piers, which have been built all around the island to reach the warm, sparkling waters beyond the seagrass.

Now Ambergris Caye has some serious competition: The **Placencia Peninsula,** a beautiful strip of dazzling white sand and susurrating palms, right on the mainland. The shallow **Placencia Lagoon,** on the inland side of the peninsula, is full of pillowy seagrass and orchid-hung mangroves, nourishing the reef's rich sealife, but the sea-facing beach is a continuous strand with excellent swimming. In the space of just a few years, hotels have sprouted along the peninsula's 23km (16 miles) of white sand beach, yet Placencia itself is still a relaxed, low-key beach town, its colorful Creole-style clapboard houses mostly built on stilts. For years, the village's principal thoroughfare was a thin concrete sidewalk, listed in the *Guinness Book of World Records* as the narrowest street in the world. The sidewalk still runs through the heart of the village, but the main highway—aka "the Back Road"—carries more of the traffic these days.

There's more to do here than just laze on the sand. Diving is superb, naturally—you can either snorkel right off the beach or go with a dive operator on an excursion out to the reef. Most resorts have their own dive shops; or try **Seahorse Dive Shop**

You may see some local creatures while kayaking in Placencia.

(www.belizescuba.com). Other popular pastimes include kayaking around the lagoon or up the mangrove-lined Monkey River, tours of the **Cockscomb Basin Wildlife Sanctuary,** exploring **Mayan ruins** at Lubaantun and Nim Li Punit, or experiencing the African-flavored Garifuna village culture at **Seine Bight.**

Belize is clearly banking on Placencia's growth as a tourist destination. A new paved highway speeds the 2-hour drive southeast from Belmopan, Belize's capital; a modern airport has opened on the southern end of the peninsula. In 2010, however, the local tourism community rejected a plan to make Placencia a cruise port. (Belize City is currently the country's only cruise stop.) The locals understand that Placencia's laidback charm is one of its greatest assets, and they're not signing that away.

(i) www.placencia.com.

✈ Placencia.

🛏 $$ **Nautical Inn,** Seine Bight Village (© **800/688-0377** or 11/501/523-3595; www.nauticalinnbelize.com). $$ **Singing Sands Inn,** 714 Maya Beach Rd. (© **888/201-6425** or 11/501/520-8022; www.singingsands.com).

Phu Quoc Long Beach
Vietnam's Saucy Secret
Vietnam

FOR MANY YEARS, RUGGEDLY BEAUTIFUL PHU QUOC REMAINED OFF the tourist radar, as Vietnam's nascent tourism industry doubted international visitors would come to a destination studded with military bases, built to fend off nearby Cambodia's territorial claims. But the tropical appeal of Phu Quoc, with miles of palm-lined white sand beach and jaw-dropping sunset views, finally won out, and the government is banking on Phu Quoc to become a worthy rival to Thailand's stunning but now-crowded Phuket.

Lying off Vietnam's west coast, Phu Quoc is constantly cooled by ocean breezes, and thus a great escape from sultry Saigon. Visit October through March to escape the monsoons that keep Pho Quoc's thickly forested interior so green (80% of the island is protected national forest). Phu Quoc was historically famous for two

A fishing village on the island of Phu Quoc, Vietnam.

things: pepper and *nuoc mam* (fish sauce). Pepper plantations are still scattered about the jungly interior, laced with red dirt-track roads and dotted with ramshackle bungalows.

The island's largest town is the fishing port of Duong Dong, on the western shore; the most resort-developed beach, the aptly named Long Beach, is close to town. But don't spend your whole time here; explore the rest of the island. Up the dusty coastal track, you'll pass small fishing villages set on salty inlets, soon reaching **Ong Lang,** about 6km (3¾ miles) north of Duong Dong, which now has a few small resorts along a quiet stretch of sand. North of there, long stretches of beach are lined with fish and squid drying on large bamboo mats, preparing you for the tangy air of **Gan Dau,** a small town full of fish sauce factories. Farther out on the peninsula, you'll find a few local hangout spots with hammocks under shade trees by the beach. At the northern end of the island, beachgoers can enter the military area to enjoy the pristine seclusion of **Bai Thom Beach.**

The coastal track south from Duong Dong leads past Duong To village (worth a stop to visit the Phu Quoc Pearl Farm) to the small seaport of **An Thoi** at the southern end of the island. This is a jumping-off point for snorkeling expeditions to the **An Thoi Archipelago,** 15 small islands and islets surrounded by deep blue waters. (For another colorful local experience, take a nighttime expedition to join the local fishing fleet to hunt for squid, which are drawn to the surface by flashlights.) Near An Thoi, beautiful **Khem Beach** is a long white-sand strand with some actual pounding surf. Popular with Vietnamese beachgoers, so far Khem has no resorts, just a few beachside sugar shacks with low tables under umbrellas. Inevitably this will change as resort development steps up; come here now and you'll be able to boast that you knew Phu Quoc in the "good old days."

✈ Phu Quoc (45 minutes from Ho Chi Minh City).

🚢 From Rach Gia (3 hr.).

🛏 $$ **Grand Mercure La Veranda,** Tran Hung Dao St, Duong Dong Beach (*©* **84/77/398-2988;** www.mercure-asia. com). $ Mango Bay Resort, Ong Lang Beach (*©* **84/77/398-1693;** www.mangobayphuquoc.com).

Beach #7 (Radha Nagar Beach)
More Than Just a Number
Havelock Island, India

HAVELOCK ISLAND CLEARLY HASN'T HIRED A MARKETING EXPERT TO name its beaches. The beach next to the island's ferry port, on the northern end, is called "Beach No. 1," and from there on they are numbered clockwise around the island. They're all lovely, but Beach No. 7, on the western coast of Havelock—close to Radha Nagar village—is so stunning, it really deserves a better name. The jungle slopes right down to Radha Nagar beach's pearl-white sands, with no civilization in sight save for a couple of palm-roofed huts selling snacks and renting snorkel fins. In peak season, January through May (avoid the monsoon months of June and July), the skies are reliably sunny, the sea calm and deep turquoise, with a few small coral reefs and great underwater visibility.

If marketing experts haven't moved in on Havelock Island, neither have chain resorts or mass-market amenities. That's one of the island's most powerful charms. Indian tourism authorities recognize that this Andaman Island haven is a jewel, offering the sort of tropical beauty you're more likely to find in nearby Thailand or Myanmar. So far, however, Havelock has been developed only minimally, with an eye to preserving its ecotourism qualities. Most of the island's small-scale lodgings and restaurants are strung along the east coast road between the villages of **Govind Nagar** (Beach #3) and **Vijay Nagar** (Beach #5); the cross island road to Radha Nagar branches west from Govind Nagar, which has just enough shops and local *dhabas* (roadside restaurants) to earn the title of "main town." To get around the island, you'll have to take a rattletrap green public bus, rent a motorscooter, or flag down one of the jaunty autorickshaws puttering about looking for fares. No roads at all go to **Elephant Beach** on the northwest shore—a prime diving spot—it's a half-hour snorkel-boat ride from the Havelock Jetty or a half-hour hike on a jungle footpath from Radha Nagar.

There are roughly 550 islands in the Andaman archipelago, which lies off India's east coast in the sweeping Bay of Bengal, but only about 25 of them are inhabited. The locals are friendly, unjaded, and laidback, even in the Andamans' capital, **Port Blair.** Despite the effort it takes to reach Havelock—the ferry from Port Blair takes 2 to 4 hours, and the one daily seaplane flight is wildly expensive—this gem of an island has become the Andamans' most visited destination, especially popular with divers and snorkelers. But bring cash with you—there's only one ATM on Havelock Island, and very few places take credit cards. Who needs plastic when you can have paradise?

ⓘ www.andamanisland.com.

✈ Port Blair (connections to Kolkata or Chennai).

🚢 From Port Blair, 2-4 hr. depending on boat.

🛏 $$$ **Barefoot at Havelock,** Radha Nagar (© **91/95660/88560**; www.diveandamans.com). $$ **Sea Shell Resort,** #2 Govind Nagar (© **91/9332/39625** or 91/3192/242773; www.seashellhavelock.com).

TOUR Andaman Holidays (© **91/3192/234924**; www.andamanholidays.com).

43

Local Color

Patara Beach
Jewel of the Turquoise Coast
Patara, Turkey

THE ROOT OF THE WORD "TURQUOISE" MEANS "TURKISH"—A FACT that seems more than coincidence when you gaze upon the mesmerizing sapphire waters along the Turkish Riviera. The area is hardly undiscovered, of course; in high season (July and August), British and German holidaymakers fill the tiny whitewashed villas of former fishing villages like Kaş and Kalkan, where a full array of restaurants and shops have sprung up to serve their needs. But paradoxically, at the resort towns the beaches are mostly tiny pebbly shingles, while only 15km (9 miles) west of Kalkan, Patara Beach offers a wide 18 km (11-mile) stretch of gleaming white sand where the resort crowds never go. While you may choose to stay in well-equipped Kalkan, a day trip to Patara makes a wonderful escape.

This beautiful strand, backed by dunes and marsh (rent a beach umbrella, as there are no real trees here to cast any shade), remains undeveloped and unspoiled for two very good reasons: The endangered loggerhead turtles who nest on its sands, and the majestic ruins of the ancient Lycian city of **Patara,** which lies just north of the beach's towering sand dunes.

The lack of crowds at Patara is at least partly explained by the effort it takes to get here. The nearest village, Gemeliş (so named to avoid confusion with Turkey's other Patara, in Cappadoccia), is 3.5km (2 miles) south of the main coastal road, and it has few tourist amenities. Another mile or so south of the village lie the ruins, with the beach another kilometer past that. If you arrive at the beach by dolmus (the local minibus-taxis), you pay nothing; otherwise, access to the beach is through the archaeological site—you pay an admission fee to hike through the ruins and past the sand dunes to the water. Don't rush too quickly past the sun-bleached stones of ancient Patara: A large hillside amphitheater, column-lined roadways, a triple-arched triumphal gate, a public bath, and elaborate tombs in its cemetery, all speak of the Lycians' wealth and culture, as admired by the Greek epic poet Homer. Imagine those marshes you pass on your way to the beach as a great harbor full of Lycian trading vessels—it must have been quite a sight.

Patara has one other claim to fame: It's the birthplace of the 4th-century Greek bishop St. Nicholas, better known as Santa Claus. Though he became famous for his good deeds down the coast at Myra (now called Demre), Patara was his childhood home. St. Nicholas is also the patron saint of sailors, which seems only appropriate as you lie on Patara's snow-white sands, watching those turquoise Mediterranean waters sparkling beyond.

✈ Dalaman Airport, (120km/75 miles).

🛏 $$ **Patara Prince,** P.K. 10, Kalkan (© **90/242/844-3920;** www.clubpatara.com). $ **Villa Mahal,** P.K. 4, Kalkan (© **90/242/844-3268;** www.villamahal.com).

Cape Cod National Seashore
New England's Most Historic Strand
Chatham to Provincetown, Massachusetts, U.S.A.

IN AUGUST 1961, WHEN PRESIDENT JOHN F. KENNEDY DESIGNATED Cape Cod's Great Beach as America's first National Seashore, an entirely new category of national park came into being. Kennedy had a vested interest in the place—he'd grown up summering on the Cape down in Hyannisport—but he also foresaw that fragile seashore landscapes need special protection. Generations of New England beachgoers have him to thank.

This stretch of Atlantic coast has plenty of historic interest: here the Pilgrims first touched American soil, Thoreau meditated on nature, countless sailing ships wrecked in the so-called Ocean's Graveyard, and Marconi's first transatlantic telegram was received. But the Seashore's real claim to fame is its beaches—in reality, one 40-mile-long (64km) beach—with dunes 50 to 150 feet (15 to 46m) high. Those awesome beaches, all well marked off of Route 6, include **Coast Guard** and **Nauset Light beaches** in Eastham, **Marconi Beach** in Wellfleet, **Head of the Meadow Beach** in Truro, and **Race Point** and **Herring Cove beaches** in Provincetown 18.

This is the Atlantic Ocean, so the surf is bracingly rough and cold (less strong swimmers may prefer a bay beach on the western side of this narrow peninsula). Admission is charged to all beach parking lots, though there's a much smaller fee for pedestrians and cyclists, making it a splendid option to arrive via the **Cape Cod Rail Trail,** which runs from Dennis to Wellfleet. Most visitors stay a full day, so parking lots fill up early. You'll hear plenty of Boston accents here, and see lots of Red Sox caps and Patriots jerseys. Tote along a cooler of refreshments, as there are no concessions (which preserves the unspoiled feel of the open strand), then do as the locals do and head for a lobster dinner after your day at the beach, with creamy New England clam chowder to start.

Marconi Beach.

Just yards away from white sand and surf lies a whole other natural world, with its own meditative rhythms: a rich wilderness of marsh and wetlands tucked away behind the beach. Here, the seashore's rangers carefully monitor endangered species like the piping plover and eastern box turtle—don't be surprised if you find sections of beach roped off during nesting season. Marked nature trails abound: The **Nauset Marsh and Buttonwood trails** at the Salt Pond Visitor Center in Eastham; the **Wellfleet Bay Wildlife Sanctuary's trails** in South Wellfleet; and the **Pamet Trail** in Truro (off N. Pamet Rd.), which winds through another uniquely Cape Codian landscape: a cranberry bog. And talk about iconic New England images—you'll find historic lighthouses strung all along this perilous coast, from **Highland Light** in Truro to the postcard-perfect red-and-white **Nauset Light** in Eastham.

ⓘ Cape Cod National Seashore (ⓒ **508/771-2144;** www.nps.gov/caco).

✈ Hyannis.

🛏 $$ **Viking Shores Motor Lodge,** 5200 State Highway (Rte. 6,) Eastham (ⓒ **800/242-2131** or 508/255-3200; www.vikingshores.com). $$ **Even'tide,** 650 State Highway (Rte. 6), South Wellfleet (ⓒ **800/368-0007** or 508/349-3410; www.eventidemotel.com).

Roundstone Beach
Windsurfing in the Wild West
County Galway, Ireland

WEST OF GALWAY CITY LIES A LAND OF "SAVAGE BEAUTY," IN THE words of Oscar Wilde. The Atlantic coastline around here is ragged, notched with hundreds of tiny inlets; inland is a vast plum-colored moorland running north to stark mountains. Driving up the scenic N59 road, park your car and just try to walk on that terrain—the ground shivers under your feet, and you discover that it's actually a waterlogged tapestry of wildflower, grasses, and mossy peat, colored in all the heathery hues of Ireland.

This is the famous **Roundstone Bog** of Connemara, the heart of Ireland's wild west, and its crown jewel is the charming 19th-century seaside village of Roundstone. Set along the coastal R341 road, its marketing slogan, "Ireland's most picturesque village," is well earned. Streets slope steeply down to its busy fishing harbor, lined with close-set pastel stucco cottages. The village's name comes from the Irish *Cloch na Rón,* meaning "seal's rock," and sure enough, you can still see that rock full of seals at the entrance to Bertraghboy Bay. Fishermen still ply their trade, but over the past few years Roundstone has also become a resort town, popular with artists and craftspeople. Pubs and seafood restaurants abound, and galleries sell beautiful hand-painted pottery, chunky silver Connemara jewelry, and the traditional goatskin-topped Irish drums known as *bodhrans.*

From the village, head about 3km (2 miles) up the Ballyconneely Road to find a gorgeous pair of sandy crescent beaches, set back-to-back on either side of a peninsula (technically, a tombola) that divides two bays, Gorteen Bay and Dog's Bay. **Gorteen** is the larger beach, curving around the western end of its bay; its calm, crystal clear waters make it a great swimming spot. The waters are a little more lively in Dog's Bay (in Irish, *Port na Feadoige,* or "bay of the plover"), which lies west of the headland. **Dog's Bay Beach**'s sand is stunningly white, formed entirely of ground shells instead of quartz; lapped by clear turquoise Gulf Stream waters, it's a good place to spot dolphins. It's also one of Ireland's most challenging windsurfing spots, with nice waves and a close chop; Gorteen Bay offers windsurfers another option, with strong winds and smooth water.

For a sweeping view, walk out onto the headland that separates the two beaches (always respecting pathways that protect the dunes, which are continually re-planted with dune grass to prevent coastal erosion). The water vista on all three sides is spectacular enough, but when you turn and see the craggy **Twelve Bens** mountains looming in the near distance, you'll catch your breath. The Wild West was never lovelier.

ⓘ www.roundstone-connemara.com.

✈ and 🚆 Galway City (80km/50 miles).

🛏 $ **Errisbeg Lodge,** R341, Roundstone (✆ **353/95/35807;** www.errisbeglodge.com). $$ **Island View House,** Roundstone Village (✆ **353/95/35701;** www.islandview.ie).

Local Color

46

Venice Beach
The People Parade
Venice, California, U.S.A.

IN A STATE LOADED WITH BEAUTIFUL EXPANSES OF GOLDEN SAND—Los Angeles County alone has 30 miles (48km) of beaches on its 72 miles (116km) of coastline, most of them public parks with full amenities—why choose Venice Beach? Yes, it has 3 miles (5km) of wide white manicured sands that slope gently into the Pacific Ocean's lapping surf. But swimming and sunbathing are almost beside the point here. The thing that really makes Venice Beach stand out from its neighbors—Marina del Rey to the south, Santa Monica ㉔

An artist at work at Venice Beach.

to the north—is the world-class people-watching it offers along its paved beachside promenade, aka **Ocean Front Walk.**

Venice Beach really is just like the movies depict it, a seemingly endless whirl of characters and misfits, flaunting their weirdness under the swaying palm trees. You'll spot outrageous outfits and bizarre pets, piercings and tattoos and hair dyed every color under the sun. Some individuals show up hoping to make a buck—buskers, sidewalk caricaturists, mimes, fortune-tellers, fire-eaters, snake-charmers, contortionists, you name it (bring a fistful of $1 bills to reward the ones you like). But other folks are just out there letting their freak flags fly, skating along the bike path, lounging on benches and concrete barriers, or browsing the funky little boardwalk stands and shops.

The intersection where Washington Boulevard meets the recently restored Venice Fishing Pier is a good place to start: Head up the beachfront from here to watch the passing show at **Skate Dancing plaza,** beach volleyball courts, skateboarding ramps (remember the movie *Dogtown and Z-Boys?*), basketball courts (remember the movie *White Men Can't Jump?*), and **Muscle Beach,** where bronzed bodybuilders (Arnold Schwarzenegger and Lou Ferigno are alumni) show off their stuff. Surfers hover offshore at the **Venice Breakwater,** just north of the Venice Pier. While there are several interesting restaurants inland from the beach (try Abbot Kinney Boulevard), the Promenade itself is more of a hot dog and juice-bar sort of venue, decidedly democratic and low-brow.

Venice Beach comes naturally by its oddball quality. Developed as a model community by Abbot Kinney in 1905, it was styled as an American version of Venice, Italy (you can still see a few canals running between its colorful bungalows) but languished in the Depression. It became a Beatnik hangout in the 1950s and has remained a community of artists, actors, musicians, and freethinkers of all stripes. When Joel and Ethan Coen needed a home address for the shaggy dropout hero played by Jeff Bridges in their classic movie *The Big Lebowski,* they didn't have to think twice. Where else would "the Dude" live but Venice Beach?

ⓘ www.venicebeach.com.

✈ Los Angeles International.

🛏 $$ **Venice Beach House,** 1 Speedway, Venice (© **310/823-1966;** www.venicebeachhouse.com). $$ **The Inn at Venice Beach,** 327 Washington Blvd., Venice (© **800/828-0688** or 310/821-2557; www.innatvenicebeach.com).

47 Local Color

Stinson Beach
Beyond the Golden Gate
North California, U.S.A.

IN THE BAY AREA, THERE'S NO GUARANTEE OF A FOG-FREE WEEKEND, even in summer. San Franciscans and Oaklanders don't wait for blue skies—they grab their towels and Frisbees, shoo the dog into the back seat, strap the kayak to the roof, and slip across the Golden Gate Bridge, heading 20 miles (32km) up scenic Highway 1 to Stinson Beach. As the car swings around the last curving descent, a foam-fringed crescent of beach suddenly sparkles into view, a panorama that virtually defines the word Beach.

Stretching for 3½ miles (5.6km) along a narrow spit enclosing the Bolinas Lagoon (a fine bird-watching spot), Stinson Beach is one of California's most popular and beautiful strands. Edged by low grassy dunes, like most Northern California beaches Stinson Beach offers a limited sort of swimming. The water is bracingly cold (an average 58°F/14°C in summer), and swimmers must be prepared for rip tides or for unpredictable large "sneaker" waves, which rush farther up the shore than expected. (Be on the lookout also for sharks, which occasionally cruise into swimming areas.) Lifeguards are on duty from May to mid-September. Part of the Golden Gate National Recreation Area, it's well-equipped with facilities such as restrooms, showers, picnic areas, and even a snack bar in summer. In summer the surf is best for rafting and body-boarding; the wave action picks up in winter and spring for more serious surfing. Windsurfers find the best winds come

Stinson Beach.

around the point in the afternoons. Only the northern end of the beach, county-run Upton Beach, allows dogs on leash.

Directly adjacent to the beach, the small town of **Stinson Beach** has a casual, laidback vibe, with a string of cafes and surf shops along the main road. The town sprang up in 1906, when refugees from San Francisco earthquake were temporarily resettled here, at the western foot of towering Mount Tamalpais; it has been a beach resort since the 1920s, though after the Golden Gate opened in 1937, Stinson Beach really came into its own as a day trip destination.

While you're here, don't miss the opportunity for a very special, and quintessentially North Californian, side trip. Turn off on the Panoramic Highway, which roughly parallels Highway 1, to **visit Muir Woods National Monument,** where you can stroll along marked trails through a hushed and tranquil grove of towering redwoods, many of them 500 years old. It's like a forest cathedral, with golden sunlight falling in long shafts through the branches to dapple a needled-carpeted woodland floor.

ⓘ ℭ **415/868-1922**; www.stinsonbeachonline.com or www.nps.gov/goga.

✈ San Francisco International (53 miles/85km).

🛏 $$ **The Sandpiper**, 1 Marine Way, Stinson Beach (ℭ **877/557-4737** or 415/868-1632; www.sandpiperstinsonbeach.com).

48 Local Color

Seven-Mile Beach
Reggae & Red Stripe
Jamaica

IN THE COMPETITION FOR TOURIST DOLLARS, MANY CARIBBEAN ISLANDS have brushed their local culture under a palm frond, grooming a face of manicured resorts and AmEx-ready amenities. Not so Jamaica. For better or worse, this island nation has stayed true to its own robust personality—a flavorful mix of jerk chicken, dread-locked Rastafarians, Blue Mountain coffee, local Red Stripe beer, the pulsing rhythms of reggae, and a "no worries, mon" mentality.

Most first-time visitors head for Montego Bay, with all its glitzy hotels, clubs, restaurants, and swarms of cruise passengers. Mo' Bay can feel a little hectic and plasticized, though—not what everyone expects from a Caribbean beach holiday. A far more colorful and relaxing choice is **Negril,** on Jamaica's far western tip, with its famously romantic **Seven-Mile Beach.** Opening onto a tranquil lagoon protected by a coral reef, the white sands of Seven-Mile Beach are set against an idyllic tropical backdrop of sea grapes and coconut palms. Clean aquamarine waters, coral reefs, and under-sea caverns make Seven-Mile Beach one of the Caribbean's best sites for diving and snorkeling. Kiosks along the beaches rent watersports equipment, from snorkel gear to jet-skis, parasails, and water skis.

The hippie crowd first popularized Seven-Mile Beach in the 1960s, lending it a reputation for pot-smoking, nude sunbathing, and general hedonism. But the area has cleaned up its act since, as big resort chains such as SuperClubs, Sandals, and Couples developed extensive all-inclusive properties in the early 1990s. You'll still see some nude sun-worshippers on Seven-Mile's white sands (most resorts specifically designate "clothing optional" areas), but the carefree spirit of the place somehow makes it seems more natural than shocking. If you want to escape the hair-braiders, aloe masseurs, hustlers, and thumping reggae beat, head for **Long Bay Beach Park** at the far northern end of Seven-Mile Beach. Out beyond the hotel belt, this stretch of beach offers picnic tables and changing rooms. Even during the busy winter months, it's often the least crowded of all Negril's beaches.

Negril's local building codes forbid the construction of buildings that rise above the canopy of trees, which mean that the resorts are invariably low-rise, blending organically into the flat, sandy landscape. The more upmarket East End—where the most substantial resorts are located—occupies either side of the highway leading into town from the east (from Montego Bay). The West End of Negril is more down-to-earth, with modest cottages, boutique-style hotels and guesthouses, and local restaurants loaded with Jamaican spirit. And isn't that what you came here for?

ⓘ www.negril.com.

✈ Negril or Montego Bay.

🛏 $$$ **The Caves,** Lighthouse Station, Negril (© **800/688-7678** or 876/957-0270; www.thecavesresort.com). $$ **Idle Awhile Resort,** Norman Manley Blvd., Negril (© **877/243-5352** or 876/957-3303; www.idleawhile.com).

Santa Rosa Island
Panhandle Sugar
Pensacola, Florida, U.S.A.

THERE'S WHITE SAND AND WHITE SAND—AND THEN THERE'S THE Alabaster white sand of Northwest Florida's Gulf shore. It's so sparkling-white and fine, it deserves a class by itself. It's made not of seashells but of ground quartz, which began as Appalachian Mountain granite, steadily eroded and carried downstream—*way* downstream—by rivers and creeks to the Gulf of Mexico.

One of the longest barrier islands in the world, Santa Rosa Island offers 50 miles (80km) of that amazing white sand, stretching along the western Panhandle of Florida near the city of Pensacola. Except for a few built-up communities at Navarre Beach and Pensacola Beach (look for a kitschy water tower painted to look like a beach ball), it's all undeveloped, protected as part of the **Gulf Islands National Seashore.** Santa Rosa is no wider than a quarter mile, a simple strip with water on both sides—nothing but serene beach, beach highway, and rolling dunes covered with sea grass and sea oats. Countless terns, snowy plovers, black skimmers, and other birds nest along the dunes, while a gentle slope of that blindingly white sand rolls into the warm emerald waters of the Gulf of Mexico.

Conveniently connected to the mainland by several bridges—at Destin, Fort Walton Beach, Navarre, and Gulf Breeze—low-lying Santa Rosa's long beach highway connects several sections of the Seashore: the open white sands of **Opal Beach,** along Route 399 between Navarre Beach and Pensacola Beach; the **Fort Pickens** section at Santa Rosa's western end, where there are campgrounds and nature trails; and the **Naval Live Oaks Area,** back on the mainland, where nature trails lead through oaks and pines to picnic areas and a beach. (The Seashore's visitor center is here.) A little jog up through Pensacola takes you to the Seashore's next barrier island to the west, **Perdido Key,** a picturesque area for canoeing or kayaking. While there are several well-developed beach resorts near here—Fort Walton, Destin, Panama City—thanks to the Seashore the Panhandle still has a laidback old Florida feel, with open skies, fishing piers, and casual roadside restaurants.

That incredible sand does have a few drawbacks. It's too fine for prime sandcastle building, for one thing. Also, there aren't many shells to gather on these beaches, which weren't formed by shells in the first place. That gradual sandy bottom, so ideal for wading and swimming, doesn't offer snorkelers much to see near shore, beyond a few sand dollars. But the water is so clear, it's worth getting out to the few offshore shipwrecks that have been turned into artificial reefs, where fish, dolphins, and loggerhead turtles play. And nobody's really complaining about the sands of Santa Rosa—they're just too beautiful.

ⓘ www.nps.gov/guis or www.visitpensacola.com.

✈ Pensacola.

🛏 $$ **Hampton Inn Pensacola Beach,** 2 Via de Luna, Pensacola Beach (ⓒ **850/932-6800;** www.hamptonpensacolabeach.com). $$$ **Portofino Island Resort and Spa,** 10 Portofino Dr., Pensacola Beach (ⓒ **877/484-3405;** www.portofinoisland.com).

Sports on the Sand 50

Trunk Bay
Trail Blazer
St. John, U.S.V.I.

WANT TO GET SOMEONE HOOKED ON SNORKELING? START OUT WITH A visit to Trunk Bay, on the northwestern coast of St. John, the gem of the U.S. Virgin Islands. Thanks to a 1956 land gift from Laurence

You might spy a sea turtle while snorkeling Trunk Bay.

Rockefeller, two-thirds of this thickly forested island is preserved as national park, and the park boundaries don't stop at the shoreline. A great deal of the surrounding reefs and water are also protected—incredibly clear, sparkling turquoise waters, truly breathtaking to behold.

Water sports are one of St. John's chief attractions, especially snorkeling and diving, given the great underwater visibility in these clear waters. Trunk Bay is ideally set up for beginners, well provided with toilets, a snack bar, and lifeguards. You can rent snorkeling gear right here at the Cinnamon Bay Watersports Center (as well as windsurfing gear—Trunk Bay is prime territory for windsurfers too).

You wade in from the fine white sands of Trunk Bay's ¼ mile-long (.4km) beach, shaded by palms and sea grape trees. Divided by a spit of land, the shallow, calm bay is punctuated by rocky **Trunk Cay,** a short swim out from the beach, so there's lots of underwater architecture to explore—all of which is interpreted by a 225-yard (206-m) signposted **Underwater Trail.** This trail zigzags along a healthy young reef where numerous features, only 5–15 ft.

(1.5–4.6m) under the water's surface, have been labeled with signs. The markers are a fantastic way for novice snorkelers—or even more experienced snorkelers who aren't up on the terminology—to learn the difference between various coral structures, or between a sea fan and an anemone. There's no way to put a label on all the fish flitting past—blue tang, yellowtail snapper, parrotfish, butterflyfish—but they're there, thriving in these protected waters. Shallow rocky areas at the edges of the bay shelter octopuses and crustaceans, and in the middle of the bay, green turtles, stingrays, and eagle rays patrol the deeper waters and soft beds of sea grass.

Once Trunk Bay has whetted your appetite, you can take your mask and fins to other choice snorkeling spots around St. John. Usually uncrowded **Leinster Bay,** on the island's north coast, offers clear, calm water and lots of brilliantly hued tropical fish. Locals favor **Haulover Bay,** on the north coast of the island's East End, where the ledges, walls, and nooks are set very close together; the waters here are extraordinarily clear, even by St. John standards. On the island's southeast tip, Salt Pond Bay attracts snorkelers as well. There won't be signposts at these other sites, but now you'll know what you're looking at.

ⓘ Trunk Bay visitor center, ✆ **340/776-6201;** www.nps.gov/viis.

✈ St. Thomas.

⛴ From St. Thomas, 20 min.

🛏 $ **Cinnamon Bay Campground,** Cruz Bay (✆ **340/776-6330;** www.cinnamonbay.com). $$$ **Westin St. John Resort,** Great Cruz Bay (✆ **800/937-8461** or 866/716-81080; www.westin resortstjohn.com).

The Baths
Boulder & Boulder
Virgin Gorda, British Virgin Islands

IT'S PROBABLY THE MOST-PHOTOGRAPHED BEACH IN THE BRITISH Virgin Islands—immense granite rocks strewn along powdery white sands, forming enchanting grottoes and hidden pools. But for those who love snorkeling, what's more interesting is the marine life that thrives under the smooth, shallow, crystal-blue waters around The Baths.

Only about 10 miles (16km) long, Virgin Gorda is edged with small tasteful luxury resorts; it's known as a sailor's paradise, with numerous protected coves where boats can anchor. For snorkelers, the good news is lots of shallow coral reefs close to shore, as well as pinnacles, ledges, and boulders that shelter all sorts of tropical fish, such as sergeant majors, blue tang, and puffer fish; green turtles and baby hawksbills bask on the edge of the sand and paddle around the sea grass.

The most popular snorkeling sites lie on the southern tip, around three adjacent beaches, all protected as one national park. Drive down the west coast from Spanish Town, Virgin Gorda's main town, stopping first at **Spring Bay,** the most easily accessed of the three beaches. With its white sand, clear water, and sandy bottom, it's the best of three for swimming, while its many tiny coves offer fine snorkeling.

The road leads on south to the **Baths**—or rather, the Top of the Baths, a cluster of bars and restaurants located by the trail that leads down to the Baths themselves, a 10-minute hike. To protect the coral reefs, sailboats must tie up only at park moorings, but The Baths is such a well-known site, its moorings are often filled to capacity. Come early to explore the place in peace: Climb around those spectacular grottoes, admiring how the rocks' striations change colors as sparkling seawater floods into the rock niches.

Then, to get away from the crowds, proceed south from the Baths' beach along a rugged trail, basically a jumble of granite boulders that occasionally requires some wading through the shallows. Passing great stands of organ pipe cactus, you'll enter **Devil's Bay,** a secluded coral beach heaped with more of those dramatic boulders. With no direct road access, fewer sightseers make their way here, so the snorkeling is much pleasanter.

If you've got very young snorkelers in your party, you may want to check out yet another cove south of Devil's Bay, called the **Crawl:** a calm shallow lagoon almost entirely surrounded by boulders where little snorkelers can explore their own small reef. There are still plenty of fish to gaze at—it's a great way to get the kids hooked on snorkeling.

(i) www.bviwelcome.com.

✈ Tortola.

🚢 From Tortola (30 min.).

🛏 **$$$ Biras Creek Resort** (© **877/883-0756** in the U.S. or 284/494-3555; www.biras.com). **$$ Nail Bay Resort,** Nail Bay (© **800/871-3551** in the U.S., or 284/494-8000; www.nailbay.com).

Sports on the Sand 52

Bonaire Marine Park
Ring Around the Reefs
Netherlands Antilles, the Caribbean

AT FIRST SIGHT, SCRUBBY BONAIRE MAY SEEM LIKE NOTHING MORE than a desert island. Its real riches, however, lie offshore, in a surrounding ring of healthy coral reefs and incredibly clear water, where visibility is often about 30m (100 ft.) or more. A couple of decades ago, as hotels first began cropping up along the ocean's

Windsurfing in Bonaire.

edge, savvy Bonaire residents had the foresight to realize that this would be their greatest tourism draw. By creating the Bonaire Marine Park, they ensured that this island would forever be known as a diver's paradise.

Beaches here tend to be small, with sharp coral underfoot—swimmers may prefer to head southeast for mangrove-lined Lac Bay, and the sandy shallows of **Lac Bay Beach** and **Sorbon Beach.** (It's also the island's best area for windsurfing and kayaking.) **Eden Beach,** just north of Kralendijk, also has a good stretch of sand, or climb down the stairs to **Thousand Steps Beach,** set below limestone cliffs on the northwest coast. (Don't worry, there are actually only about 75 stairs to navigate.)

On the other hand, you never have to go far for a dive site. Painted yellow rocks along the coastal roads point the way to some 60 shore dive sites. Regulars all have their own favorite snorkel spots—more popular include **Thousands Steps, Tori's Reef, Karpata** (when it's calm), **Andrea 1,** and **Windsock.** The Marine Park incorporates the entire coastline plus the tiny offshore island of Klein Bonaire. It also provides permanent dive-site moorings (since anchoring on coral is a big no-no), rangers to police the reefs and enforce regulations, and services and facilities including a visitor center, the Karpata Ecological Center, at the entrance to Washington Slagbaai Park on the island's northwest end.

Whether you're diving, snorkeling, windsurfing, or just swimming, you'll pay a small annual fee to enter Bonaire's protected waters; tags are available from any dive shop. Though scuba diving is a big focus—many operators offer PADI instruction—guided snorkeling tours are also readily available: Contact Bonaire Dive and Adventure (www.bonairediveandadventure.com) if your resort's dive operator doesn't offer one. Even the shallow reef ledge is full of marine life, with over 355 species from beautiful parrotfish and damselfish to outsize groupers and tough-looking moray eels. The variety of coral formations attracts a corresponding variety of fish: At 1m (3¼ ft.) you can find brain coral; at 3m (9¾ ft.) you begin to see staghorn and elkhorn coral and the graceful, swaying, feathery soft-coral "trees" known as gorgonians. Bonaire also has a huge population of sea turtles, which you are likely to encounter—don't swim directly above them, in case they need to surface for air.

ⓘ Bonaire Marine Park (ⓒ **599/717-8444;** www.bmp.org, www.infobonaire.com).

✈ Bonaire.

🛏 $$ **Divi Flamingo Beach Resort,** J.A. Abraham Blvd. 40, Kralendijk (ⓒ **800/367-3484** or 599/717-8285; www.diviflamingo.com). $$ **Eden Beach Resort,** Kaya Gobernador N. Debrot 73 (ⓒ **599/717-6720;** www.edenbeach.com).

West Bay Beach
Barefoot Charmer
Roátan, Honduras

ROÁTAN IS THAT RARE THING: AN AS-YET UNSPOILED CARIBBEAN island, with pristine sugary-sand beaches, lush tropical greenery, and warm, friendly islanders. Perhaps more to the point, it sits on the second-largest barrier reef in the world, a gorgeous strand of coral bedecked with vivid tropical fish, eagle rays, turtles, and sponges, much of it protected as a marine park.

Located off the Caribbean coast of Central America, Roátan is the largest of the Bay Islands, a cove-notched crescent of land 65km (40 miles) long and only 127 sq. km (49 sq. miles) in area. Not surprisingly, divers and snorkelers were among the first to "discover" Roátan, prizing its warm clear waters and varied underwater topography, an interesting mix of ridges, channels, and vertical walls, with a few shipwrecks as well to explore. Some 130 dive sites circle the island, and numerous reliable dive shops can get you onto the reef in under 30 minutes. (A few dive-centered resorts have their own facilities right on the property.) Perhaps the densest concentration of sites, however, lies along the pristine protected reef of the marine park, on the northwest coast from Sandy Bay down to West Bay. Swimmers and snorkelers gravitate to the West Bay for another reason: it has the island's best white-sand beaches, where you can wade straight into the calm shallow waters and head for the reef.

Roátan's vibe is laid back and relaxed, the sort of place where divers needn't worry about dressing up or coping with crowds. What nightlife there is mostly consists of hanging out in shorts and T-shirts, sharing your day's adventures with new island pals; you're more likely to be nursing a sunburn than a hangover. As an alternative to water activities during the day, try out the jungle canopy tours at **Gumbalimba Nature Park** (www.gumbalimbapark.com), a forested jungle reserve filled with colorful tropical birds like parrots and native macaws.

How long Roátan will remain so easygoing and unspoiled is anybody's guess. At the moment, its lodging is mostly small inns and hostels, along with resorts that cater mostly to divers. But more upscale resorts are in the wings, direct flights from the U.S. are increasing, and both Royal Caribbean and Carnival cruise lines are greatly expanding their Roátan arrivals. Best advice: Come here now before everybody else does.

ⓘ www.roatanmarinepark.com.

✈ Roátan.

🛏 $ **Bananarama Dive Resort,** West Bay (✆ **504/2445-5005;** www.bananaramadive.com). $$ **Mayan Princess Resort,** West Bay (✆ **504/445-5050;** www.mayanprincess.com).

Sports on the Sand

54

Black Rock Beach
Kaanapali Monopoly
Maui, Hawaii, U.S.A.

ON MAUI, YOU CAN HAVE YOUR CAKE AND EAT IT TOO: PAMPERING full-service resorts and luxuriant white-sand beaches as well as world-class diving and snorkeling. With abundant reefs, both natural and artificial, the clear warm waters of Maui are blessed with a profusion of marine life, including many species found nowhere else. Snorkel purists wouldn't dream of leaving Maui without booking a dive boat for a trip to the islet of **Molokini,** which is really the lip of a submerged crater that provides a natural sanctuary for tropical fish. Excursions down the rugged south coast to the black-lava coves of **Ahihi-Kinau Natural Preserve** and **La Pérouse Bay** are also worth rising early for.

But some days, you just want to take your mask and fins and wade in off the beach. And those are the days when you should head for **Kaanapali Beach,** on the west Maui coast just north of historic Lahaina.

Four-mile (5km)-long Kaanapali is one of Maui's best beaches, with grainy gold sand as far as the eye can see. The beach parallels the sea channel through most of its length; the surf is placid and the sand powdery and warm. It's hardly a secluded spot—a paved beach walk runs the length of the beach, linking several large resort hotels and condos, open-air restaurants, and Whalers Village shopping center. What you lose in seclusion, however, you gain in convenience: You can rent all sorts of water sports gear from vendors in front of the hotels, and you can easily find parking in the hotel lots, though you'll have to pay for it. But because Kaanapali is so long, and because most hotels have adjacent swimming pools, the beach is crowded only in pockets—there's plenty of room to find some quiet sandy spot for yourself.

And at the north end of this busy beach, you'll find a prime snorkeling destination: the aptly named **Black Rock,** a rocky peninsula jutting out into the clear blue ocean in front of the Sheraton Maui Resort. Where you first wade in, the water is only about 8 feet (2.4m) deep, with a nice sandy bottom; it gets deeper as you go further around the point. Protected by an underwater lava rock ledge, the waters here are calm and clear, and swarming with tropical fish: butterfly fish, parrotfish, trigger fish, needlefish—damsels and wrasses and tangs, oh my! You might even spot a turtle or two, or endemic Hawaiian fish like the Humuhumunukunukuapuaa. All those sunbathers down the beach have no idea what they're missing.

(i) www.visitmaui.com or www.gohawaii.com.

✈ Kapalua-West Maui.

🏨 $$$ **Sheraton Maui Resort and Spa,** 2605 Kaanapali Parkway (📞 866/500-8313 or **808/661-0031;** www.sheraton-maui.com). $$ **Kaanapali Beach Rentals** (📞 **800/887-7654;** www.kaanapalibeachrentals.com).

Cabarete
Catch the Wind
Dominican Republic

FOR SUN-SEEKING NORTH AMERICANS AND BRITS, CHEAP PACKAGE getaways to the Dominican Republic's resort-packed Coconut Coast have long been a quick solution to the winter doldrums. Nonstop flights from the U.S. to Santo Domingo make it even do-able to spend a weekend basking in the sun on the crowded white-sand beaches of Punta Cana.

But a youthful crowd of adrenaline addicts have more recently established their own beachhead on the D.R.—Cabarete, on the less-traveled north coast. For them, life in Cabarete revolves around three things: windsurfing or kiteboarding, partying, and resting up to hit the water again.

Few places provide such ideal conditions for active watersports. A coral reef protects the entrance of Cabarete's bay, keeping its water relatively smooth, while verdant low-lying hills behind the village create a thermal effect with incoming trade winds. Waves break at 1 to 2m (3–6 ft.) and the winds are consistently around 25 to 30kmph (15–20 mph). Canadian windsurfing pro Jean Laporte first discovered Cabarete's perfect conditions in 1984; the resort town you'll find here today sprang up in the early 1990s after Laporte spread the word. Frequent sporting events, such as the Kiteboarding World Cup and the Red Bull Masters of the Ocean event, draw pros as well as spectators here; there are two prime seasons, December to April and June to August.

Because Cabarete grew quickly, don't expect traditional charm: along Calle Principal (the coastal highway) there's a utilitarian scrum of shops, small hotels, bars, and restaurants. What really counts is what lies north of the road: **Playa Cabarete,** a 3km-long (2-mile) coconut-palm-lined curve of blushing sand continually lapped by foam-edged waves. While the surfers congregate west of town at **Playa Encuentro,** the kiteboarders gather along **Bozo**

Beach, where the main beach begins to curve northward, catching those sturdy winds, or **Kite Beach** at the western end of the bay. Several watersports companies are based here. Beginners may want to take kiteboarding lessons from Laurel Eastman Kiteboarding (www.laureleastman.com) or learn windsurfing from the Cabarete Windsports Club (www.cabaretewindsportsclub.com).

Cabarete's primary visitors are not only young and athletic, they tend to be European, many hailing from France, Holland, Germany, Poland, and Bulgaria. (A growing number of French and German expatriates have settled here full-time.) There's a definite countercultural vibe, a sort of Endless Summer devotion to sun, fun, watersports, good times, and hard drinking. Some of that may change as developers eye beautiful Cabarete as a potential site for large-scale resorts. Right now, though, those colorful kites hovering over the turquoise bay have the sky to themselves.

ⓘ www.godominicanrepublic.com or www.activecabarete.com.

✈ Santo Domingo.

🛏 $$ **Velero Beach Resort,** Calle La Punta (ⓒ **809/571-9727;** www.velerobeach.com). $ **Kitebeach Hotel,** Carretera Sosua (ⓒ **809/571-0878;** www.kitebeachhotel.com).

56 Sports on the Sand

La Digue
Digue It
The Seychelles Islands

FROM THE AIR, IT LOOKS LIKE A SPRINKLING OF PEARLS IN A SEA OF ethereal blue—the 115-island archipelago of the Seychelles, floating in the West Indian Ocean some 1,800km (1,118 miles) from Kenya's east coast. Thanks to air travel, the Seychelles aren't as isolated as they used to be, but they're still not a cheap easy getaway. You must fly into the largest island, Mahé, and then take smaller planes or boats on to other islands; there are limited accommodations on most islands, and they're usually expensive. Nevertheless, for idyllically beautiful beaches and oceans teeming with marine life, it's pretty hard to beat the Seychelles.

Once you're here, a little island-hopping is essential. Even casual snorkelers feel compelled to put on a mask and fins, with eternally warm waters (the Seychelles lie only 4 degrees south of the equator) and protected marine reserves on 14 islands. From Mahé you can take a full- or half-day trip out to the six tiny islands of the **Sainte-Anne Marine Park,** where thousands of colorful fish, sea turtles, and bottlenose dolphins share the water with you. But why go halfway when you've already flown this far? Fly over to **Praslin** island and then catch a ferry to the small granite island of **La Digue,** the Seychelles fourth largest island—and some say, the most beautiful.

La Digue has a leisurely, old-world pace—you can walk or bike anywhere, and locals still depend on oxcarts for transportation. Coconut palms, Indian almond trees, and takamaka trees shade the roadsides, and forests are hung with delicate orchids and fragrant vanilla vines. But La Digue's great claim to fame is the stunning white-sand beaches that ring its coast, with rugged granite formations off shore. Chief among them is **Anse Source d'Argent,** on the western coast, with its dramatic jumble of black-streaked pink granite boulders, featured on countless magazine covers.

Anse Source D'Argent isn't just pretty to look at; it also offers some excellent snorkeling around those rocks, where shafts of sunlight dance over branching coral and rainbow-hued tropical fish. Nearby, on the southwest coast, the beaches of **Anse La Reunion** and **Anse Union** are also prime snorkeling sites, as well as **Anse Patates,** on the island's northernmost point. Or hire a boat to visit one of La Digue's satellite islands—the marine reserve of **L'Ile Coco** is a great choice—with their pristine reefs and coves.

The ferry from Praslin only takes 20 minutes, but resist the urge to make La Digue a day trip. Why miss a chance to watch the sun set over those spectacular beaches? And tomorrow morning, those turquoise waters will be waiting all over again.

ⓘ www.seychelles.travel.

✈ Mahé.

🚢 From Praslin, 20 min.

🛏 $$ **Patatran Village,** Anse Patates (ℂ **248/29 43 00;** www.patatranseychelles.com). $$$ **Le Domaine de L'Orangeraie,** Anse Sévère (ℂ **248/4299 999;** www.orangeraie.sc).

Tarifa
Tilting at Windmills
Spain

LOOK ACROSS THE STRAITS OF GIBRALTAR AND YOU CAN SEE THE green hills of Morocco—that's how close to Africa you are in Tarifa. Surrounded by mountains, this laidback Andalucian seaport at Europe's southernmost tip—where the Mediterranean Sea empties into the Atlantic Ocean—just may have the windiest beaches in the world. Those big white wind turbines spinning on the hills above town make up the largest wind farm in Europe. And ever since windsurfers first found their way here in the 1980s, Tarifa has been celebrated as Europe's year-round windsports capital.

Climatologists explain the Tarifa phenomenon as a combination of offshore levanter and onshore poinente winds, intensified by the rocky hillsides. (Hang-gliding and rock climbing are also popular here.) Several villages in the Tarifa area attract windsurfers and surfers, as well as aficionados of those newer sports, kiteboarding and stand-up paddle surfboarding, and all along the sandy coastline between Tarifa and Conil to the northwest, a surf-bum infrastructure has sprung up, with simple hostels and posadas, nondescript village cafes, and open-air fish grills.

SPORTS ON THE SAND

Tarifa, Spain.

To the immediate south of Tarifa, the white sands of **Playa de los Lances** stretch for 5km (3 miles) along the Atlantic. Sought out by surfers for its high winds and strong undertow, unspoiled Playa de los Lances is a protected natural area with nearby wetlands. Another popular spot for windsurfing is **El Porro en Ensenada de Valdevaqueros,** the bay formed by Punta Paloma to the immediate west of Tarifa. Continue northwest on the E-5 to the white-walled hamlet of **Zahara de los Atunes,** where an athletic crowd of youthful Europeans congregates to windsurf off the beach of **Playa Zahara. Playa El Palmar,** near Conil, is sandy but treeless, with whipping winds. To rent equipment or book lessons, contact Tarifa Spin Out Surfbase (www.tarifaspinout.com), Dragon Kite School (www.dragonkiteschool.com), or Volare Tarifa Center (http://tarifa windsurfing.com). These local shops can also update you on current wind conditions, which will affect which beach you choose.

Tarifa is still not overrun with resorts or tourist crowds; its winding, cobbled streets with flower-filled patios still seems more like a Moorish fishing village than a modern resort destination. White-washed houses terrace down the hillsides, and you can see traces of the old fortified city walls. The nightlife here is thoroughly modern, however—and the sports crowd takes full advantage of that, too.

✈ Gibraltar.

🚢 From Tangiers, 35-45 min. (www.frs.es).

🛏 $$ **Hotel Hurricane,** Carretera Nacional 340, Km 78 (✆ **34/956/68 49 19;** www.hotelhurricane.com). $$ **Hotel Dos Mares,** Carretera Nacional 340, Km 79.5 (✆ **34/956/68 40 35;** www.gmares.com/dosmares).

58 Sports on the Sand

Playa El Yaque
Freestyle Heaven
Isla de Margarita, Venezuela

ISLA MARGARITA WAS ONCE KNOWN AS THE "PEARL OF THE CARIBBEAN" for the pearl-rich oyster beds that Christopher Columbus discovered nearby in 1498. Those beds are sadly long gone, plundered by treasure-mad conquistadors. But this slightly raffish island off of Venezuela's northeastern coast has developed into a pearl of a different sort, with gorgeous sugary beaches, warm breezes, and turquoise seas attracting an increasing number of tourists.

Popular as it is with South Americans, Isla Margarita is still largely undiscovered by North Americans, with one exception: watersports enthusiasts who flock to **Playa El Yaque,** on the south side of the island near the airport. Once a small fishing village, the powdery white crescent of El Yaque was colonized in the late 1990s by Canadian windsurfers, who first discovered its perfect conditions. El Yaque's waters are shallow and warm, but even more important are the steady side winds that blow year-round, thanks to an airstream funneled between Isla de Margarita and its island neighbor Coche. Rainfall is a rarity, and the weather is warm year-round (average temperature 31°C/88°F, with water temperatures in the 77°F/25°C range); the winds are most favorable from January to June. The days follow a predictable pattern: Light morning winds favor beginners, then gradually pick up strength until the wind peaks at 25 to 30 knots by mid-afternoon, giving more advanced windsurfers a decent run for their money. (Kiteboarders congregate at a separate upwind area, known as Kite Beach, reachable by shuttle boat.) The waters are flat and shallow near shore, becoming choppy about 400 meters out; past the reef line, a certain amount of rolling swell offers some bump-and-jump action. Freestylers in particular appreciate El Yaque's flat waters, which give them scope for all sorts of maneuvers. (Several of the world's leading freestylers are El Yaque regulars.)

In general, the tourism infrastructure on Isla de Margarita is loose and laidback—call it earthy South American charm—but in El Yaque, things are even more carefree, with stray dogs and cats roaming the streets and street vendors hawking their wares on the beaches. You'll have no trouble renting gear or finding lessons, for windsurfing and kiteboarding outfits line the beachfront, alternating with pleasantly scruffy bars and cafes. Most lodgings are composed of a smattering of apartments around a small swimming pool, with clean, basic rooms, at very un-Caribbean prices—a perfect set-up for the beach bum lifestyle.

ⓘ www.margarita-island-venezuela.com.

✈ Caribe Santiago Mariño airport, Porlamar (40 min. from Caracas).

🛏 $ **Hotel Atti,** Calle Principal (✆ **58/295/263-9850;** http://hotelatti.com). $ **El Yaque Paradise,** Calle Principal (✆ **58/295/263-9810;** www.hotelyaqueparadise.com).

Sports on the Sand **59**

Newquay
Magical Mystery Tour
Cornwall, England

DOWN AT ITS SOUTHWESTERN TIP, ENGLAND TURNS WILD—RUGGED, wind-buffeted, and wave-lashed. The mossy castles of Arthurian legend and gabled waterside inns out of *Treasure Island* are its classic postcard images; sooty mining towns and steep cobble-stoned fishing villages reflect its traditional industries. Yet in the past few decades, as the seas were fished out and the mines closed, tourism has become Cornwall's bread and butter. And no wonder—with nearly 485km (300 miles) of rocky Atlantic coastline, warmed by the Gulf Stream, Cornwall has some of the U.K.'s best beaches and most dynamic surf.

The heart of watersports action is **Newquay,** on Cornwall's north coast. The "New" quay that the town is named after was built in 1439, but never mind—these days Newquay attracts everyone from bronzed surfers to sandpail-toting families to elderly ladies who summer in quaint harborside B&Bs. With several fine sandy beaches, sitting on sheltered bays at the foot of rugged Cornish cliffs, Newquay has been a holiday resort since the late 19th century. The Beatles' *Magical Mystery Tour* was supposedly a day trip to Newquay. It's got plentiful hotels and tourist attractions—a zoo, a miniature railway, lovely town gardens, and (most important for surfer types) plenty of bars and music clubs.

Surfers have taken over broad sandy **Fistral Beach,** just west of town on Fistral Bay, home base for the British Surfing Association and site of the annual Boardmasters Festival. Backed by sand dunes, Fistral Beach faces west—which means it catches strong Atlantic swells, bringing waves averaging up to 5m (15 ft.) in winter. At the north end of the beach, a reef called the Cribbar creates monster wave breaks of as high as 12m (40 ft.). You'll need a wetsuit, a good idea even in summer, when the waves are a quarter that size and better for beginners.

Watersporters also head 3.2km (2 miles) north of town to **Watergate Bay,** where northwesterly exposure and constantly shifting sand banks keep the wave action varied. Along with surfing, paddle-surfing and kiteboarding are popular here, along with the newest extreme sport, waveskiing. (Contact Extreme Sports, www.watergate.co.uk, for equipment and lessons.) Instead of trying to balance while standing upright on a board, the basic premise of waveskiing is to surf sitting down, using a sort of kayak-surfboard crossbreed. You put your legs straight ahead of you, buckle up (those waves can get bumpy), and use your paddles as rudders to navigate the waves. The learning curve isn't as steep as it is for surfing, but paddling into major swells brings the same kind of adrenaline rush.

ⓘ www.visitnewquay.org and www.cornwalltouristboard.co.uk.

✈ Newquay Cornwall Airport.

🚃 Newquay, 6½ hr. from London.

🛏 $$ **Headland Hotel,** Fistral Beach (ⓒ **44/1637/872-211;** www.headlandhotel.co.uk). $$ **Hotel Bristol,** Narrowcliff (ⓒ **800/ 528-1234** or 44/1637/875-181; www.hotelbristol.co.uk).

Sports on the Sand 60

Laguna Beach
Skimming the Waves
Laguna Beach, California, U.S.A.

WHAT'S THE GUY DOING OUT THERE ON THE SPARKLING BLUE PACIFIC Ocean? He's twisting, spinning, jumping, and flipping like no surfer you've ever seen, and now—riding his board backwards—he's sliding straight onto the sands of Laguna Beach.

With its dramatic coastal headlands and 7 miles (11km) of fine-grained white sand beaches, Mediterranean-flavored Laguna Beach is just as handsome as its neighbor to the north, Newport Beach ❹. But when it comes to skimboarding, Laguna is way more than just another pretty So Cal beach town. Skimboarding was actually invented here, as you'll see from old 1920s-era photos of Laguna Beach lifeguards skimming across the sand on large plywood boards. The sport has greatly advanced since then, thanks to high-tech modern boards made of fiberglass or carbon fiber wrapped around high density foam. Though it's definitely a niche sport, it has gradually spread around the world, with skimboarding enclaves in Cabos San Lucas, Mexico; Dewey Beach, Delaware; and around Cape Hatteras ❻ in North Carolina. Nevertheless, Laguna

Beach is still the center of the skimboarding universe; many pro skimboarders live here, and skimboard manufacturers such as Victoria Skimboards make it their base. It's also the site of the annual **Victoria Skimboards World Championships,** an invitational event for qualified amateurs and pro riders.

In contrast to surfing, prime skimboarding conditions require waves that break close to shore, which suits Laguna's beaches perfectly. Sidewashes, powerful shorebreaks, and rocky reefs make many of the town beaches better for surfing and skimboarding than for swimming—notably **Brooks Street, Thalia Street,** and **St. Ann's** in the center of town, as well as **Crescent Bay** to the north and **Treasure Island** to the south. Almost every kid who grows up in Laguna Beach has at least tried to skimboard, hooked early by watching the hotshots perform.

You can do lots of cool tricks on a skimboard, which is typically smaller and thinner than a surfboard. Unlike surfing, skimboarding starts on the sand—a skimboarder waits for the right wave, then runs toward the ocean to drop his or her board on the thin layer of receding water. As the tide withdraws from shore, the skimboard almost hydroplanes along the surface of the water, sliding out to reach the breaking waves. At that point, the skimboarder shifts his or her weight and direction and rides back to shore, much as a surfer might do.

Skilled skimboarders can ride down the line like a surfer, or launch off the wave and do aerial tricks, such as a Wrap, a Superman, or a Coffin (lying on one's back on the skimboard with feet facing straight out). Just watching the hotshots can get your pulse pumping—and just wait till you try it yourself!

ⓘ www.skimonline.com or www.lagunabeachinfo.com.

✈ John Wayne Airport, Orange County (15 miles/24km).

🛏 $$$ **Montage Resort & Spa,** 30801 South Coast Hwy. (ⓒ **866/271-6953** or 949/715-6000; www.montagelagunabeach. com). $$ **Casa Laguna Inn & Spa,** 2510 South Coast Hwy. (ⓒ **800/233-0449** or 949/494-2996; www.casalaguna.com).

Cape Hatteras
Bank on It
The Outer Banks, North Carolina, U.S.A.

THE GRAVEYARD OF THE ATLANTIC, THEY USED TO CALL IT. SHIPWRECKS litter the Atlantic along this 70-mile (133km) strip of barrier islands, feared by mariners for its treacherous waters, shifting shoals, powerful rip tides, and summer thunderstorms that sweep in at a moment's notice. But for modern windsurfers and kiteboarders, that combo of powerful winds and waves is downright irresistible.

For windsurfers, in fact, the only problem in the Outer Banks is deciding where to go. Do you want the relatively flat, chest-deep shallows of protected Pamlico Sound west of the islands, or the Atlantic swells and onshore winds on their eastern side? Conditions depend upon many factors—which quarter the wind is blowing from, where the swells are, where new sandbars have risen, or how the tide affects the Sound's depth. There are so many launching points—with colorful names (Ego Beach, Kill Devils Hills, Canadian Hole, Buxton Slick) or almost mythical tags (the Cove, the Point, the Lighthouse, Ramp 34)—it's best to network with locals and/or the many excellent windsurf outfitters before picking a site. Spring and fall are the prime windsurfing seasons, but locals windsurf happily year-round, always finding some new challenge in these ever-changing waters.

If the winds aren't favorable, Hatteras's Atlantic shore has some of the most consistent surf breaks on the East Coast, while the Sound offers excellent wakeboarding. The Sound is also good for kayaking; adrenaline junkies may even want to try ocean kayaking. In summer, kiteboarding comes to the fore, making the most of Pamlico Sound's smooth shallow waters and steady robust winds. (Novices can learn the basics at the Kitty Hawk Kiteboarding Resort, www.kittyhawkkites.com, in Rodanthe.) Those winds are key—after all, there was a reason why the Wright Brothers came all the way from Ohio to fly their aircraft on the Outer Banks beach at Kitty Hawk.

Repeat visitors are hooked on the land's-end vibe of the Outer Banks, its edgy wind-scoured beauty and promise of drama. Laced together by Highway 12, the Outer Banks runs from the Northern Beaches peninsula (from Duck to Nags Head) on to Bodie Island, Hatteras Island, Ocracoke, and Cedar Island, much of which is the **Cape Hatteras National Seashore.** (The towns of Rodanthe, Waves, Salvo, Avon, Buxton, Hatteras, and Ocracoke lie within, but are separate from, from the national park.) Cape Hatteras is an informal, barefoot hangout, where it's easy to beach-hop—just pull into one of many beach-access parking lots, cross a small board-walk over dunes of sea oats, and plop down in the tawny sand.

ⓘ www.outerbanks.org.

✈ Norfolk Intl (80 miles/129km).

🛏 $$ **Cape Hatteras Bed & Breakfast,** 4223 Old Lighthouse Rd., Buxton (✆ **800/252-3316** or 252/995-6004; www.cape hatterasbandb.com). $$ **The Inn on Pamlico Sound,** 49684 Hwy. 12, Buxton (✆ **866/726-5426** or 252/995-7030; www.innonpamlico sound.com).

62 Sports on the Sand

La Jolla Cove
California Streaming
San Diego, California, U.S.A.

IN A GALLERY OF U.S. STATE FISHES, CALIFORNIA'S ENTRY—THE Garibaldi fish—is quite the star act, with its gaudy neon-orange scales and plump foot-long body. What a trip it would be to see one of these overgrown goldfish flashing through the open water! Well, there's one place you can—the clear, calm waters of La Jolla Cove.

Garibaldis aren't the only fish that snorkelers see in this rocky, protected cove in the gorgeous San Diego suburb of La Jolla. Yellow tails, silvery sardines, rockfish, perch, stripey smelt, dotted

opaleyes, brown-patterned kelp bass, colorful starfish, crabs, and bat rays skim through the waters; you may even spot the endangered giant black sea bass. Harmless leopard sharks patrol the shallows, while California gray seals laze around nearby Children's Pool, and dolphins drift over from the kelp beds offshore.

While surfers primarily think of La Jolla in terms of famed surf sites Windansea Beach and Bird Rock, the snorkeling here is just as stellar. Top-notch snorkeling sites are rare in California, but several factors bless La Jolla Cove—its north-facing orientation, the rocky headlands that block the Pacific surf, a strategically located pair of artificial reefs built 30-plus years ago. La Jolla has a Mediterranean-like microclimate (temperatures rarely dip below 50°F, or 10°C), and while the water isn't exactly balmy, it does climb past 70°F/22°C in summer—feasible swimming temperature, with great visibility (up to 30 ft./10m). Perhaps most importantly of all, La Jolla Cove's offshore waters are a boat-free protected area, the Ecological Reserve, established in 1971 as part of the **San Diego-La Jolla Underwater Park,** which stretches for 10 miles (16km) up the coast to Torrey Pines. Several local outfitters lead snorkel tours of the Reserve. You can enter the water either from the small beach in La Jolla Cove itself (enter from the cul-de-sac off Coast Boulevard) or from the gently sloping sands of La Jolla Shores (take Torrey Pines Road to La Jolla Shores Drive). From the cove, you can also head north to explore the La Jolla Sea Caves.

This marine reserve is connected to the famous **Scripps Oceanographic Institute,** which was founded in 1903 in a boathouse on Coronado Island ⓪, but moved in 1905 to the bluffs that rise above unspoiled La Jolla Cove. (Today, the green lawns of Scripps Park sweep along those bluffs, a great place for a breathtaking coastal stroll at sunset). The Scripps Institute is now based a short distance up the coast; visit its **Birch Aquarium** at 2300 Exposition Way to see the fish that eluded you in the Cove.

✈ San Diego International.

🛏 **$$ Best Western Inn By the Sea,** 7830 Fay Ave., La Jolla (ⓒ **800/526-4545** or 858/459-4461; www.bestwestern.com/innby thesea). **$$ Inn at the Park,** 525 Spruce St., San Diego (ⓒ **877/499-7163** or 619/291-0099; www.parkmanorsuites.com).

The North Shore
Hawaii's Triple Threat
Oahu, Hawaii, U.S.A.

EVERY DECEMBER, THE PROFESSIONAL SURFERS' SEASON ENDS HERE, with the Hawaiian Triple Crown—three surf competitions held on renowned beaches in the birthplace of surfing. As you watch those giant swells roll in from the north Pacific, curling over into tubes before crashing on sandy beaches, you realize why the ancient Hawaiians *had* to develop surfing into an art.

Three hotspots line the Kamehameha Highway north of Haleiwa, a funky town infused with surfer vibe. The first you'll come to is **Waimea Beach Park,** where the Quicksilver Big Wave Invitational is held every winter, provided the waves are over 20 feet (6m)—which has only happened eight times since 1984. This tournament is held in memory of Eddie Aikau, the fearless championship surfer who saved countless lives as Waimea's first lifeguard. (In surfing lingo, the phrase "Eddie would go" has come to mean "don't back away from challenging conditions.") This deep sandy bowl is placid in summer, but in winter waves pound narrow Waimea Bay, sometimes rising to 50 feet (80) high. People drive from all over Oahu just to gawk at the monster waves.

A short drive further north, Ehukai Beach Park actually has three beaches. The first one as you enter, long broad **Ehukai Beach,** offers excellent sandbar surfing for body and board surfers. But the real action begins 100 yards to the left, at **Pipeline,** where a shallow coral shelf creates such steep waves that their crests fall forward, forming a near-perfect tube, or "pipeline." Riding that tube above the shallow reef, where the water's only 6 feet (2m) deep, is devilishly difficult—the first surfer to ride Pipeline successfully was Phil Edwards in the early 1960s, and even today, Pipeline causes plenty of injuries and even fatalities. Just west of Pipeline, popular

Waimea Beach Park, Oahu.

"Banzai Beach" earned its name in the late 1950s, when film-maker Bruce Brown (later of *Endless Summer* fame), cheered on a bodysurfer by yelling "Banzai!," a Japanese toast for good luck. Ever since, surfers can't resist yelling "Banzai!" as they ride this beach's huge curling waves.

The North Shore's third major beach lies just north of Ehukai: **Sunset Beach,** known for its thundering 15- to 20-ft. (5- to 7m) waves and dangerous rip currents (the "Sunset rip"). Sunset's huge sandy beach is right by the street, so it's a great place to people-watch, attracting not only surfers but sunbathing beauties and camera-toting tourists.

Note that these landmark breaks are for experienced surfers only—beginners should learn the sport down near Waikiki ❶, and simply admire the North Shore pros from the beach. Curiously enough, the surf action happens only in winter (Oct–Apr)—the rest of the year, these same beaches transform into placid spots for swimming and snorkeling. Needless to say, the surfers will have already moved on.

www.visit-oahu.com.

Honolulu International.

$$$ **Turtle Bay Hilton,** 57-091 Kamehameha Hwy., Kahuku (© **866/827-5321** or 808/293-6000; www.turtlebayresort.com). $$ **Ke Iki Beach Bungalows,** 59-579 Ke Iki Rd., Haleiwa (© **866/638-8229** or 808/638-8229; www.keikibeach.com).

Surfing Meccas **64**

Isla Todo Santos
Killer Reputation
Mexico

JUST AN HOUR'S DRIVE SOUTH OF THE CALIFORNIA/MEXICO BORDER, tiny Isla Todos Santos doesn't seem like much—a pristine rocky islet in the Bay of Ensenada, where no one lives except for shorebirds, sea lions, and harbor seals. But surfers make that drive south every winter because of what lies off Todos Santos Island's northwest tip: a reef break so notorious, it has earned the name "Killers."

Here in the bracingly cold Northern Baja waters, incoming Pacific swells are doubled in size by a deep underwater canyon, and the surf spits out monster waves as high as 15m (49 ft.). At "Killers," they've been known to reach 60 ft (18m) or more, thanks to a reef that points directly into the mouth of those oncoming swells. First discovered in the early 1960s by surfers from La Jolla, these giant waves have earned Todos Santos Island such prestige that it now draws big-time competitions, including those leading up to the Billabong XXL Global Big Wave awards. Yet Killers is a very makeable wave for confident, competent surfers. Summer and fall are considered the best seasons.

Since Todos Santos Island is uninhabited, you need a boat to get there. Most people base themselves in northern Baja's sport-fishing hotspot, **Ensenada,** where the local *pangas* (skiffs) do a brisk business in taking surfers across the 15km (10 miles) of open water to the island. Bring everything you'll need—food, drink, sunscreen, and so on—because there are no facilities on the island itself. In most cases, you need to be towed to the big reef breaks, where you'll anchor and paddle into the lineup. If Killers seems too crowded—and it does get crowded when the waves are good—check out the other breaks on the island, such as **Thor's Hammer** or **Chicken's,** which is in the channel between the two halves of Todos Santos Island, Sur and Norte (south and north). To get the lowdown, and to rent any equipment you didn't bring with you, check out Ensenada's **San Miguel Surf Shop** (Avenida Lopez Mateos, between Gastelum and Miramar).

(i) www.visitmexico.com.

✈ Tijuana or Ensenada.

🛏 $$ **Estero Beach Resort,** Estero Beach, Ensenada (© **52/ 646/176-6225;** www.hotelesterobeach.com). $$ **Las Rosas Hotel and Spa,** Carretera Tijuana-Ensenada, Ensenada (© **800/6440165** or 52/646/174-4320; www.lasrosas.com).

65 Surfing Meccas

Uluwatu
The Surfers Temple
Bali, Indonesia

MACAQUE MONKEYS SWARM ALL OVER THE STONE CARVINGS OF THE ancient mossy Javanese temple of Uluwatu. With its stunning clifftop setting on rugged Bukit Peninsula, which hangs off the southern end of Bali, it's an exotic scene indeed. But most visitors to Bali, Indonesia's largest tourist attraction, are here instead for plush white sands and pampering resorts. Before tourism really took off, there weren't even paved roads to Uluwatu.

But that never stopped the surfers. Ever since 1972, when Albert Falzon's surf movie *Morning of the Earth* opened with a shot of Uluwatu's pink cliffs and curling waves, this Indonesian beach (Salubuan is its official name) has been a magnet for adventure-loving surfers. And while tourism to Bali has mushroomed since then, getting to Uluwatu still feels like an adventure—the roads may be paved but they twist and turn, and it's a steep 5-minute hike down to the beach. Riding the waves there is more adventure still.

There are four different sections at Uluwatu. The **Peak,** set right in front of a sea cave, has a consistent set of short and powerful waves, best at high tide. When the tide's low, move to adjacent **Racetrack,** which has super-fast waves and relatively easy barrels. You should also wait for low tide to try Uluwatu's most renowned break, **Outside Corner,** with long fast waves that don't even begin to crest until the swell is at least 2.4m (8 ft.) high. Only experts should attempt **Temples,** with its long and hollow wave, because the waters there are perilously shallow.

The beach itself at Uluwatu isn't outstanding—a coral-edged strip of sand and shingle at the foot of the cliffs. A cluster of *warungs* (small open-air cafes) perch on the cliffs overlooking the waves; these are your best vantage point for watching the experienced surfers riding the waves (not to mention phenomenal sunset views). While you're here, you may also want to check out nearby **Padang Padang,** known for its heavy, dangerous waves, and **Bingin,** with its flamboyant tube-riding off a seriously gorgeous (and so far undeveloped) golden beach. Surfing outfitters will organize an itinerary for you to visit several breaks while you're here: Try **Tropicsurf** (www.tropicsurf.net) or check out www.surftravel online.com. Note that Bali's surfing season traditionally runs from April to November, which is when Uluwatu's waves are at their best; the rest of the year, the action moves to Bali's less-famous east coast beaches.

✈ Kuta International Airport, Bali.

🛏 $$$ **Alila Villas Uluwatu,** Jalan Belimbing Sari, Uluwatu (© **62/361/848-2166;** www.alilahotels.com). $ **Mu Bungalows,** Bingin Beach (© **62/361/895-7442;** www.mu-bali.com).

Malibu

American Classic

California, U.S.A.

HOW MANY SURFING BEACHES CAN BOAST THEIR OWN NAMESAKE surfboard? It's called the Malibu Board, and it's the quintessential classic longboard. But then, when you think about it, Malibu has also had a car named after it (the Chevy Malibu, 1964) and a guitar (the Fender Malibu, 1965). Music, cars, and surf—that trifecta of American coolness pretty much sums up Malibu.

In 1926, when Tom Blake and Sam Reid became the first to surf off of Malibu Point (today known as Surfrider Beach), they had to sneak onto the land, which was a private ranch. But ranch owner Rhoda May Rindge was already luring movie stars to her new Malibu Beach Motion Picture Colony, whose first residents included Ronald Colman, Bing Crosby, Gary Cooper, and Gloria Swanson; celebrities have favored Malibu ever since. Surf culture added to Malibu's allure, and it really took off in the 1950s. Set in Malibu, the 1957 novel (and 1959 film) *Gidget* taught Americans surfer lingo like "hang-ten"—a move whereby a surfer hangs all ten toes over the front of his board. (The best board for "hanging ten" is a Malibu board, by the way.)

Malibu's glamorous image and proximity to Los Angeles—it's just a short shoot up the Pacific Coast Highway (PCH) from Santa Monica **24**—mean that its prime surf spots, **Surfrider Beach** and **Zuma Beach,** are often jam-packed, and the water's usually rough, gray, and cold. Nevertheless, the quality shape of its waves makes Malibu surfing a perennial favorite.

Tucked between Malibu Pier and the Malibu Lagoon, south-facing Surfrider Beach (exit PCH at Serra Rd.) is an iconic surf break, full of takeoff spots and lively waves. Surfers subdivide it into **First Point** (closest to the pier, generally better for beginners), **Second Point,** and **Third Point** (closest to the lagoon). Occasionally you'll get a 12-ft. (4m) wave here, although 2- to 4- ft. (.6m- to 1.2-m) is

123

A surfer catches a wave in Malibu.

more common, but curls are well-shaped, and even small waves give good rides.

Farther up the PCH (turn off 1 mile/1.6km past Kanan Dune Road), roomy **Zuma Beach County Park** offers 3 miles (5km) of white sand, loaded with amenities—snack bars, restrooms, volleyball courts, and some fantastic sunbathing, in front of Malibu Colony's pricey homes. Its swells are fairly consistent, but the waves are short and quick, not necessarily good for learners. To escape the crowds, head south to the section known as **Westward Beach,** shielded by sandstone cliffs.

On your way into town, check into the town's two venerable surf shops, right on the PCH just south of Malibu Pier—the **Malibu Surf Shack** (22935 PCH; www.malibusurfshack.com) and **Zuma Jay Surfboards** (22775 PCH; www.zumajays.com). Zuma Jay himself is also Malibu's new mayor. How many surf towns can boast having a surfer in the mayor seat?

(i) www.malibucomplete.com.

✈ Los Angeles International.

🛏 $$ **Casa Malibu,** 22752 Pacific Coast Hwy. (📞 **310/456-2219**). $$$ **Malibu Beach Inn,** 22878 Pacific Coast Hwy. (📞 **800/462-5428** or 310/456-6444; www.malibubeachinn.com).

67 Surfing Meccas

Witches' Rock
Roca Bruja
Costa Rica

COSTA RICA REALLY IS AN *ENDLESS SUMMER* SORT OF PLACE—THE waters are warm year-round, with two coastlines to choose from (Pacific and Caribbean), giving the country as many as 50 prime surf destinations. The whole spectrum is represented: point breaks, beach breaks, perfect lefts, perfect rights, you name it. In this eco-friendly country, the sand and water are reliably pristine, and with so many other surfers gravitating here, you'll find plenty of funky cheap accommodations and knowledgeable surf shops.

Serious surfers seem compelled to try **Playa Pavones,** in a tiny beach town south of Golfitos on the Pacific coast, which is said to have the world's longest left-breaking wave. **Tamarindo,** on the central Pacific coast, promotes itself as a surfer mecca, though the town may have grown too quickly for its own good; the beach in Tamarindo itself is good for surfing beginners, while day-trips from Tamarindo to places like Playa Grande and Playa Guiones offer more challenge.

But when visiting surfers start to get that "been there, done that" feeling, there's still a sense of adventure about heading up the Pacific coast to Santa Rosa National Park, in northern Guanacaste province. The main attraction: **Witch's Rock,** or in Spanish, Roca Bruja. The namesake rock is a rugged hulk rising out of the water off the grey sands of **Playa Naranjo;** when waves crash upon it, it lets off such a roar, locals imagined that a sea witch must live inside. With its 6.5km (4-mile) stretch of beach break, at high tide Witch's Rock offers fast hollow right-breaking waves, as well as some good lefts when the swells are a little smaller. It's surrounded by wilderness, although you can drive here using a 4x4 vehicle through the park's dense tropical dry forest (in surf season, Dec–Apr, the rains haven't yet turned the park's roads to mud). Camping is allowed at the beach for those who'd like to give Witch's Rock a couple days. Many surfers, however, come here by boat—surfing charters out of Playas de Coco take about 45 minutes. Arriving by water will allow you to add a visit to the otherwise inaccessible **Ollie's Point,** also in the park. (Time it so you surf Ollie's Point at mid-tide, Witch's Rock at high tide.) Ollie's Point is named for former U.S. national security adviser Oliver North, who showed up here during the 1986 Iran-Contra scandal to support covert Contra activity in nearby Nicaragua. It was well off the beaten path then, and it still is.

ⓘ www.visitcostarica.com and www.crsurf.com.

✈ Liberia.

🛏 $ **Villa Del Sol,** A.P. 52-5019, Playa del Coco (✆ **866/793-9523** or 506/8301-8848; www.villadelsol.com). $ **Hotel La Puerta del Sol,** Calle, Playas del Coco (✆ **506/2670-0195;** www.lapuerta delsolcostarica.com).

Witches' Rock.

Jeffreys Bay
The Joys of J-Bay
South Africa

IN MANY WAYS, JEFFREYS BAY—BETTER KNOWN IN THE SURF WORLD as J-Bay—is the ultimate surf town. An easy hour's drive southwest from Port Elizabeth, it lies at the rugged western tip of Jeffreys Bay, an arc of sand, rock, and offshore reef that funnels Indian Ocean swells into spectacular waves. From June to August, surfers paddle out to join the line-ups along numerous sections of beach, waiting for those perfect waves. Surf shops line up along Da Gama Road, and an international crowd of scruffy suntanned surfers wanders in and out of the town's bars, cafes, and affordable beach-side hotels.

Surfing came late to J-Bay, not until 1964, but the surf hippies didn't have the place to themselves for long—not after the 1966 documentary *Endless Summer* and 1978's *Fantasea* sealed J-Bay's reputation as one of the world's premier point breaks. Today the main attraction is **Supertubes,** site of the Billabong Pro WCT competition every July. On the right day Supertubes' waves are 1 to 3m (4–8 ft.) high, though 4m (12 ft.) is not unknown. More importantly, they form a fast, near-perfect break, riding all the way down the beach from the point to the car park. Everyone wants to try his or her luck at Supertubes, and local surfers have little tolerance for those who don't show respect as they're waiting in the line-up.

But we're talking ultimate surf town here—when competition ties up Supertubes, surfers can still find plenty of action. At the top of the coastal strip, **Magnatubes** offers challenging (often just plain gnarly) heavy waves, best at high tides with northwest winds. Next to it, **Boneyards** has a quick hollow right reef break, with occasional lefts; the shallow water requires skill to avoid injury, hence the name. Note that territorial locals come here to escape Supertubes' crowds, and they don't always welcome outsiders. On the other side of Supertubes, **Impossibles** earned its name from its unpredictable waves; when undersea conditions are right, though, there's a great long barrel here. Next comes popular **Tubes,** where the waves are fun and barrelly, if short, with a strong rip current and small take-off section. Beyond Tubes, J-Bay's original 1960s surf site, **Point,** has a long, mellow, playful wave; even at low tide, there are rideable waves here. Young surfers (aka grommets) cut their teeth at Point while waiting to graduate to Tubes and Supertubes. The youngest beginners start out at **Main Beach,** which has no rocks and decent sandbars; one section of Main Beach, known as **Kitchen Window,** has a mellow reef break that's worth seeking out at mid-tide.

Wherever you choose to surf, remember that J-Bay's best surfing (June–Aug) happens during South Africa's winter—be sure to bring your wetsuit.

ⓘ www.jeffreysbaytourism.org.

✈ Port Elizabeth (75km/47 miles).

🛏 $$ **Diaz 15,** 15 Diaz Rd., Jeffreys Bay (✆ **27/42/293-1779;** www.diaz15.co.za). $$ **On the Beach Guesthouse,** 32 Waterkant St., Jeffreys Bay (✆ **27/42/293-3427;** http://onthebeachjbay.co.za).

69 Surfing Meccas

Bell's Beach
Riding the Surf Coast
Victoria, Australia

AUSTRALIA'S PASSION FOR SURFING DATES BACK TO 1915, WHEN THE champion Hawaiian waterman Duke Kahanamoku dazzled spectators, riding the curling waves of Freshwater Beach, near Sydney in Queensland. Today, the highrise-lined Gold Coast boasts 70km (42 miles) of surfing beaches and several epic point breaks. But many surfers claim that the heart of Australian surfing now rides the Southern Ocean swells near Melbourne—along the eastern Great Ocean Road, aka the Surf Coast.

Surfworld Museum.

The capital of the Surf Coast is Torquay, 94km (58 miles) south-west of Melbourne, home of famous **Bell's Beach.** Local surfers in the 1950s, spotting marvelous 6m-high (10 ft.) right-breaking waves off this reef-rocky point, hired their own bulldozer to dig a dirt road to the water. Bell's fame was cemented in 1962 when its annual Eastertime surfing contest was launched. Now called the Rip Curl Pro, it's the world's longest-running surfing competition. Bells Beach was named the world's first surfing recreation reserve in 1971; as a protected marine park, it even has a World Heritage listing. Only the most experienced surfers attempt Bell's, or other famously challenging breaks in Torquay such as **Winkipop, Thirteenth,** or **Reef Point.** There are, however, several Torquay surf spots that are good for all surfers, like the beach break of **Front Beach** (aka Cosy Corner), or the fun long rides at **Torquay Point.** You can also while away some time in the extensive **Surfworld Museum** (Surf City Plaza, Beach Rd.; www.surfworld.com.au), which has interactive exhibits on surfboard design and surfing history and inspiring videos of the world's best surfers.

Just west of Torquay, you'll find manageable waves at fast right-breaking **Steps** and the sandy beach break of **Jan Juc,** although the short fast hollows at **Bird Rock** require more caution. Next down the coast, **Point Impossible** isn't impossible at all, but a lively right-breaking spot with short fast waves, although it gets very crowded. Continuing down the road, the sandy beach breaks at **Anglesea** and nearby **Fairhaven** are an excellent choice for beginners.

At the fun, laidback surf town of Lorne (45 min. from Torquay), stop at the **Ozone Milk Bar** on Mountjoy Parade, a classic Australian milk bar—a kind of down-market cafe that sells everything from shakes and pies to newspapers. Lorne has the whole spectrum of surf spots, from the challenging (experts only) rocky reef-break of S.A., to classic right-breaking swells off **Lorne Point,** to the easy waves off the sandy beach of **Lorne.** Past Lorne, the Ocean Road gets truly thrilling, twisting along a cliff edge until you arrive at **Apollo Bay,** a pleasant, rarely crowded beach break where the surf is almost always up.

✈ Melbourne (94km/58 miles).

🛏 $$ **Great Ocean Road Cottages,** 10 Erskine Ave., Lorne (📞 **61/3/5289 1070;** www.greatoceanroadcottages.com). $$$ **Cumberland Lorne Resort,** 150 Mountjoy Parade, Lorne (📞 **61/3/5289 4444;** www.cumberlandlorneaccommodation.com.au).

70 Surfing Meccas

Fuerteventura
The Wind at Your Back
Canary Islands, Spain

WINDSURFERS DISCOVERED FUERTEVENTURA FIRST——ITS NAME TRANSLATES to "strong wind"—and when you feel the summer trade winds whipping through this Canary Island, in the east Atlantic off the coast of Africa, you'll understand why. Surfing didn't really begin to catch on here until the 1990s. Up to then, nearby Tenerife, the largest and most built-up of the Canaries, got most of the surfing market. But as Tenerife grew crowded with package tourists and the party crowd, surfers fled to more affordable, relaxed Fuerte, and soon discovered that its world-class breaks surpassed Tenerife's. Who knew?

With 3,000 hours of sunshine a year, and temperatures consistently between 64°F (18°C) and 75°F (24°C), Fuerte has an ideally balmy climate. No less than 152 beaches ring the coastline of this long, skinny island, yet it's not heavily developed—in fact, it's unspoiled enough to have been named a UNESCO biosphere reserve in 2009. There are still several unridden beaches just waiting to be explored.

Big waves hit the west and north coasts in autumn and winter, when the major Atlantic swells come in. A dirt road—optimistically known as the North Track—connects several good areas from Corralejo to El Cotillo; you may need a 4x4 to get to all of them. The easygoing resort town of Corralejo, on the island's northeast tip, makes a good place to start, with its long stretch of fine white dunes protected in a national park. Here you'll find three of the best known surf breaks: **Rocky Point** (Punta Helena), a right-hand reef break; the corresponding left-hand reef of **Harbour Wall** (El Muelle), with its powerful fast ride; and another left reef break at **Shooting Gallery,** so named for its fast hollows.

When Corralejo gets crowded, though, you may want to move around the tip and move south down the northwest coast. **Generosa** offers a fun, fast left-hand reef with a long wall. At the village of Mechihonas, **Mejillones** gets big waves with tricky shifting peaks; nearby **Suicides** gets fewer surfers, for good reason—the shallow waters at the reef break can be dangerous. In the small fishing village of **Majanicho,** a long righthander offers some nice challenges at low to mid-tide. There are three popular spots at **El Hierro**—the famous **Bubble,** known for its intense right-hand hollows; the long powerful double-peaked left at **Hierro;** and **German Rights,** named after the Germans who frequent its long right-handed break. You'll end up at the village of **El Cotillo,** where a long sandy beach offers many varying peaks.

The windsurfers are still here, of course, along with sailors and kite-surfers, particularly in the spring and summer. But Fuerteventura has room enough for all.

(i) www.fuerteventura.com.

✈ Fuerteventura.

🚢 From Tenerife, Las Palmas, and Gran Canaria; www.trasmediterranea.es.

🛏 $$ **Barceló Corralejo Bay,** Avenida Grandes Playas 12, Corralejo (📞 **34/928/536 050;** www.barcelo.com). $$ **Las Marismas de Correlejo,** Calle Huriamen s/n, Correlejo (📞 **34/928/537 228;** www.lasmarismascorrelejo.com).

71 Surfing Meccas

Santa Cruz
Cruising Through Santa Cruz
Santa Cruz, California, U.S.A.

AT THE NORTH END OF MONTEREY BAY, RIGHT WHERE THE NORTHERN California coast makes a sharp eastward curve, big Pacific waves roll in from the west and northwest. And as they slide past the headlands into Monterey Bay, the surfers of Santa Cruz are there, perched on their boards, waiting.

Santa Cruz deserves its nickname, "Surf City." At some point while you're here, you'll want to watch the pros shredding waves off Point Sant Cruz at the famous **Steamer Lane,** although given its dangerous break—and the territorial attitude of the regulars—you may want to go elsewhere to catch a wave yourself. Located in the old lighthouse on Lighthouse Point, the fascinating **Santa Cruz Surfing Museum** (701 West Cliff Dr.) chronicles the sport's history since the day in 1885 when three Hawaiian princes, riding carved redwood boards, rode Santa Cruz's curls for the first time.

Santa Cruz is more than just a surf town. Since 1907, Santa Cruz has also drawn families with its **beachfront amusement park** (www.beachboardwalk.com), a charmingly retro ½-mile (.8km) strip

of rides, shops, and restaurants. Two of the park's rides are national landmarks: The **Carousel of Delight,** built in 1911 with hand-carved wooden horses and a brass-ring grab; and the red-and-white **Giant Dipper Roller Coaster,** built in 1924, which offers great views of Monterey Bay from its peaks. There are lovely redwood forests just a couple miles) inland, and a 2-mile (3km) paved walking path along West Cliff Road, ideal for admiring sunsets.

But with 29 miles (47km) of beaches to offer, Santa Cruz can keep everybody happy. The wide main town beach along Beach Street is lively with beach volleyball and kids building sand-castles; the strand continues east to the Harbor (Seabright Beach, Harbor Beach) and on to the warmer waters of Twin Lakes State Beach. Along East Cliff Drive, a number of stairways lead down to beaches, including another surfer magnet, **Pleasure Point Beach.** Note that the aggressive break at 30th Street is for elite surfers only; the break at 36th Street has a greater variety of longboard waves for surfers of all levels.

West of the wharf, West Cliff Road heads out past **Cowells Beach,** which has long gentle waves that are a better choice for the less experienced surfer. Around the point at **Natural Bridge State Park** (www.scparkfriends.org), surfers can sometimes find excellent conditions just south of the rock arch. Follow the stunningly scenic Coast Road (Hwy. 1) north from town to find relatively uncrowded **Bonny Doon,** a major surfing spot near the town of Davenport, or drive an hour up the coast to **Half Moon Bay** **81** to try out the famously wild **Mavericks** break. The problem in Santa Cruz isn't finding a beach—it's deciding which one to visit today.

(i) www.santacruzca.org.

✈ San Francisco International (77 miles/124km).

🛏 $$ **Fern River Resort,** 5250 Hwy. 9, Felton (© **831/335-4412;** www.fernriver.com). $$ **Edgewater Beach Motel,** 525 Second St. (© **888/809-6767** or 831/423-0440; www.edgewater beachmotel.com).

Sagres
Land's End
Southwest Portugal

O FIM DO MUNDO IT WAS ONCE CALLED—"THE END OF THE WORLD"— a rocky escarpment jutting fiercely into the Atlantic Ocean at the extreme southwestern tip of Europe. For centuries, Europeans believed that when the sun set off Sagres, it plunged over the edge of the world. Standing on these wind-buffeted cliffs is an exhilarating experience—and hardly the kind of thrill you expect from the Algarve, Portugal's most popular tourist destination.

Famed for its balmy climate, more like North Africa than Europe (the very name comes from the Moorish Al-Gharb), the Algarve used to be a picturesque landscape full of lemon and fig trees, almond and olive orchards. Yet since the mid-1960s, unchecked resort development has filled the Algarve with boxy high-rises, crowded marinas, and environmentally inappropriate golf courses, utterly transforming its once-small fishing villages. You need to keep driving west, past the historic Moorish port of Lagos, to finally find "the real Algarve," an untamed landscape of sheer red and yellow sandstone cliffs, wave-hollowed hidden grottoes, and quiet cove beaches. Out here, your fellow tourists are more likely to be backpackers and surfers than sybaritic sunbathers.

The town of Sagres itself lies nestled between two headlands, facing onto the Bay of Sagres. Several protected white-sand beaches fringe the Sagres peninsula, although swimmers should note—no surprise—that the waters can be cold and rough. The closest beach to town, **Mareta** lies sheltered in the lee of **Sagres Point;** east of town, a steep descent takes you to small sandy **Tonel** beach. Windsurfers may prefer the beaches west of town, near the Baleeira fishing harbor: **Praia da Baleeira** and expansive **Praia do Martinhal.** Experienced surfers will want to continue a

The lighthouse at Cabo de São Vicente.

few minutes up the coast to the long beach at **Beliche.** The southern coastline, between Lagos and Sagres, attracts divers, with a number of underwater caves and (mostly) 20th-century shipwrecks; contact **Blue Ocean Divers** in Lagos (www.blue-ocean-divers.de) to organize your outings.

Given its dramatic situation, it's no surprise that Sagres played a pivotal role in Portugal's Age of Exploration. The 15th-century prince Henry the Navigator based himself here, hiring cartographers to chart the African coast and launching deft little caravels from the port at Lagos to venture into those new waters. There's little trace of Henry left in the reconstructed 16th-century fortress that now occupies that stern headland, but a giant compass dial laid out in pebbles in the courtyard pays tribute to his legendary "school of navigation" (probably a figment of historians' imagination). For another dose of lands-end adventure, take a bus 5km (3 miles) north from Sagres town to gaze out to sea from the powerful lighthouse at **Cabo de São Vicente.** It's even farther west than Sagres—end of the world, indeed.

✈ Faro International, Faro (119km/74 miles).

⊨ $$$ **Romantik Hotel Vivenda Miranda,** Porto de Mós, Lagos (© **351/282/763-222;** www.vivendamiranda.com). $$ **Pousada do Infante,** Ponta da Atalaia, Sagres (© **351/282/620-240;** www.pousadas.pt).

Escape the Crowd **73**

Loutro
Where Zorba the Greek Danced
Crete

FROM MID-JULY THROUGH AUGUST, A CRUSH OF PACKAGE-TOUR VISITORS descends on Crete, Greece's largest island. Pouring in via cruise ship and ferry and charter jet, they spread out along the coast, to nightlife-busy towns like Malia and Hersonisos and Agio Nikolais,

A waterside cafe in peaceful Loutro.

where massive concrete hotel complexes shoulder each other along water's edge. Perhaps it was only natural that resort developers should have originally targeted the north coast, with its broad sandy beaches on the Sea of Crete, facing the Grecian mainland. But these days, to find a more authentic Crete, you'll have to head south across the rugged mountainous interior to the more unspoiled coastal towns along the Sea of Libya.

Building a highway along this mountainous coast was too challenging, so a string of south coast towns from Paleohora to Hora Sfaklion found a typically Cretan solution: ferry service. The village of **Loutro** has no road access whatsoever; it's reachable only by ferry (15 min. from Sfakia) or by the E4 walking trail, which traces old goat paths along the shoreline's cliffs.

Set around a tiny sheltered bay at the end of Cape Mouri, peaceful Loutro is a charming huddle of white-washed buildings surrounding a small fishing harbor. Once the ancient city of Finikas, later the winter port of the town of Sfakia, Loutro means "bath" in Greek, probably referring to various baths whose ruins have been discovered in the surrounding hills.

Loutro does have tourist facilities, but it is mostly low-key and oriented to outdoor activities—kayaking, fishing, hiking around the steep scrubby hillsides, and (increasingly popular) outdoor yoga sessions. There is a small if somewhat gritty beach right in town; pebbly **Pervolaki Beach** and **Timios Stavros Beach** are within a few minutes' walk. But for a full day's relaxation on a beautiful sand beach, you can take a boat to various other nearby beaches: **Sweetwater** to the east, or **Marmara** or **Phoenix** beaches to the west.

Take a day trip by ferry to the tiny islet of **Gavdos** and you may be escorted by dolphins, which seem to be everywhere along this coast (no wonder the ancient Minoans had so many dolphin motifs in their art). Or you can take a day hike up into the dramatic **Imbros Gorge,** where wild thyme perfumes the grassy slopes. All the day-trippers will be herding through the famous Samaria Gorge to the west—you'll have Imbros gloriously to yourself.

ⓘ www.loutros.gr.

✈ Iraklion (160km/99 miles) or Chania (96km/60 miles).

🛏 $$ **Oasis Hotel,** Loutro (ⓒ **30/28250/91017;** www.oasis hotelloutro.com). $$ **Hotel Porto Loutro,** Loutro (ⓒ **30/28250/ 91433;** http://hotelportoloutro.com).

Escape the Crowd

74

Caladesi Island
Blue Ribbon Beach
Florida, U.S.A.

EVERY YEAR, FLORIDA GEOLOGIST STEPHEN LEATHERMAN, AKA DR. Beach, publishes a list of America's top beaches. Every year, Caladesi Island is right up there in the top 10—or at least it was until 2008, when Caladesi was named the #1 beach in America. Because of its win, it's now officially retired from competition.

Considering how many fine beaches there are along this Tampa-St. Petersburg coast, what makes Caladesi so special? For one thing, it's uninhabited and undeveloped—a breath of fresh air among the densely built-up string of barrier islands fringing the St. Pete peninsula. Its calm, shallow waters are extraordinarily clear, much clearer than the next island to the south, the one actually named Clearwater. Its 4-mile-long (6km) gulfside beach is dazzling white sand that's remarkably pristine, and because it isn't raked daily like so many resort beaches are, you can find all sorts of unusual shells.

As for sun-worshipping hordes, you won't find them on Caladesi, despite all Dr. Beach's accolades—you can't get here except by boat, and the number of visitors is purposely kept low. Only 62 passengers at a time can come over on the small ferry from neighboring Honeymoon Island, and they are only allowed to stay 4 hours; if you arrive on your own boat, you can moor at the marina at the island's north end, but with only 108 slips, it tends to fill up in high season.

Caladesi (Spanish for "beautiful bayou") once was the southern half of the unromantically-named Hog Island, until a 1921 hurricane severed it in two. Honeymoon Island, the other half, is now connected to the mainland by the Dunedin Causeway, but Caladesi was left cut off by water. That isolation turned out to be Caladesi's strongest asset. Now a state park, Caladesi has been provided with a few useful amenities, clustered near the marina—picnic tables, showers and restrooms, a playground, a cafe, and a beach concession, where you can rent kayaks and canoes for exploring the mangrove forest on the other side of the island. Walkways have been built through the dunes, preserving their fragile ecosystems of sea oats, wildflowers, and palm trees; there's also a marked nature trail through the pine flatwoods of the interior (keep your eyes peeled for ospreys, armadillos, and gopher tortoises).

But on the whole, it's a quiet, unpruned bit of beachy wilderness, which makes it extremely popular with shorebirds—American oystercatchers, black skimmers, royal and least terns, Wilson's and piping plovers—and the water birds that frequent the mangroves, including pelicans, egrets, roseate spoonbills, and herons. Loggerhead and green turtles nest on the beaches, too. It's the perfect antidote to the Tampa metrosprawl, so close and yet so totally different.

ⓘ Caladesi Island State Park (✆ **727/469-5918;** www.florida stateparks.org/CaladesiIsland).

✈ Tampa International (20 miles/32km).

🛥 20 min. from Honeymoon Island State Park (Caladesi Island Connection, ✆ **727/734-1501**).

🛏 $ **Barefoot Bay Resort & Marina,** 401 E. Shore Dr., Clearwater Beach (✆ **866/447-3316** or 727/447-3316; www. barefootbayresort.com). $$ **Sheraton Sand Key Resort,** 1160 Gulf Blvd., Clearwater Beach (✆ **800/325-3535** or 727/595-1611; www. sheratonsandkey.com).

Cumberland Island National Seashore
Just You & the Birds
Southeastern Georgia, U.S.A.

IT TAKES SOME EFFORT TO REACH THIS BARRIER ISLE AT THE SOUTHERN end of the Georgia coast, practically into Florida—unless you've got your own boat, you'll have to take a 45-minute ferry ride from St. Mary's. Once you get there, you may be surprised to find its gleaming sands deserted. What kind of a national seashore is this?

But that's all part of Cumberland Island's subtle charm. Originally a sea cotton plantation and then a summer retreat for tycoon Andrew Carnegie's family, Cumberland Island has been mostly uninhabited since 1972, with only a few private owners remaining in clustered compounds. Over the years, the wilderness has gradually closed in, until the main road through the interior seems a mere tunnel through a vine-draped canopy of live oaks, cabbage palms, magnolia, holly, red cedar, and pine. Only 300 people are allowed on the island at any given time, many of them overnight guests at the island's only lodging, the stately turn-of-the-century Greyfield Inn. (There are also two simple campgrounds for more bare-bones visitors.) Although there are a few historic sites to visit—a restored Carnegie mansion, a tiny African-American meetinghouse—most visitors tend to be nature-lovers, fond of hiking (there are over 50 miles/80km of hiking trails), bird-watching around the tidal flats, bicycling along the old carriage roads, and kayaking through the silent salt marshes.

Cumberland's sloping 16-mile-long (26km) beach isn't just a bland strip of powdery sand, like some manufactured oceanfront resort: Little meadows nestle between the dunes, creeks cut their way to the sea from freshwater ponds, and tidal mudflats glisten. It runs the entire length of the island, affording plenty of space for beachgoers to find their own secluded areas. It's not a place to come for high-octane watersports, but shell-hunting is superb, especially early in the morning after a storm. The waters are relatively shallow and calm for swimming, although there are no lifeguards. Nor are there snack bars, showers, or changing rooms—it's just you, the sand, and a wide-open sky.

Those who return to Cumberland Island year after year do so for its unhurried pace, a lifestyle attuned to the rhythms of nature. It's not a place to visit in a hurry, barging in and then charging out. Give yourself a day or two to slow down, breathe the salt air, and get sand between your toes—you'll be glad you did.

(i) www.cumberlandisland.org. Cumberland Island National Seashore, St. Mary's, GA, ✆ **912/882-4336 ext. 254;** www.nps.gov/cuis.

✈ Jacksonville FL (30 miles/48km).

🚢 45 min. from St. Mary's, reservations ✆ **912/882-4335** or 877/860-6787.

🛏 $$$ **Greyfield Inn, Cumberland Island** (✆ **866/401-8581** or 904/261-6408; www.greyfieldinn.com). $ **Sea Camp or Stafford campgrounds,** call ✆ **912/882-4335** or 877/860-6787 for reservations.

---

76 Escape the Crowd

Chappaquiddick Island
Chappy Happy
Martha's Vineyard, Massachusetts, U.S.A.

SUMMER PEOPLE AND YEAR-ROUNDERS—IN MOST RESORT AREAS, they never mix. Not so on Martha's Vineyard, a summertime magnet for the rich and famous, from James Taylor, Paul McCartney, and Bill Murray to Bill Clinton and Barack Obama. After all, many year-round Vineyarders started out as summer people themselves, and fell so in love with its oak-scrub landscape and salt-tang air that they ended up "going native."

The more important divide really lies between long-time summer people and short-term visitors. The Regulars groan about the traffic snarls in Oak Bluffs and Vineyard Haven whenever the ferries arrive from Cape Cod, and to keep day-trippers at bay, many beaches require a town resident sticker (displayed as a badge of honor on car windows). When summer gridlock sets in, the sticker-deprived masses have to hustle to find parking to visit the two big public beaches, mile-long State Beach on Vineyard Sound between Oak Bluffs and Edgartown, or, below Edgartown, 3-mile-long (5km) South Beach, with its tall white dunes and Atlantic surf.

Few visitors, however, ever get to the unspoiled beaches of Chappaquiddick Island. Lying across a narrow strait at the eastern end of the Vineyard, accessible only by a tiny ferry (the "On Time") from Edgartown Harbor, Chappaquiddick is unfortunately forever associated with the midnight car wreck in 1969 that ended the presidential ambitions of Senator Ted Kennedy. Yet this sparsely populated island full of ponds and nature preserves makes a great escape from the "mainland."

Some 5 miles (8km) from the ferry—not a bad bike ride on this flat, windswept terrain—a long golden barrier beach lies along Chappy's eastern edge, with freshwater ponds behind it, Nantucket Sound before it. The surf can be rough and the currents strong, but it's great for wading and wave jumping. The section further south, called **Wasque Beach,** is a ½ mile-long (about 1km) and has all the amenities—lifeguards, parking, and restrooms. To its north, **East Beach** runs for 7 miles (11km) up to the **Cape Pogue Lighthouse.** It has no facilities; pack a picnic if you plan to stay long. (Pack that picnic before you get to Chappaquiddick, which has only one general store.) Most people park near the Dyke Bridge (the site of Kennedy's crash) and walk the couple hundred yards on boardwalks out to the beach.

Both beaches are part of the 200-acre (81 hectare) **Wasque** (pronounced Way-squee) **Reservation,** which requires a $3 parking fee and $3 per person entrance fee. But that also means you've got a nature preserve adjacent to the beach—follow winding trails through the sand barrens, where you may spot osprey, great blue herons, and swans around Poucha and Swan Ponds. Not a bad trade-off at all!

✈ Martha's Vineyard Airport.

🚢 Oak Bluffs, Vineyard Haven, or Edgartown; ferries run from Woods Hole (✆ **508/477-8600;** www.steamshipauthority.com), Falmouth (✆ **508/548-9400,** www.falmouthferry.com; or ✆ **508/548-4800,** www.islandqueen.com), or Hyannis (✆ **800/492-8082;** www.hy-linecruises.com).

🛏 $$ **The Edgartown Inn,** 56 N. Water St., Edgartown (✆ **508/627-4794;** www.edgartowninn.com). $$ **Wesley Hotel,** 70 Lake Ave., Oak Bluffs (✆ **800/638-9027** or 508/693-6611; www.wesleyhotel.com).

77 Escape the Crowd

Barbuda
Pink Pearl
Antigua & Barbuda

UNDISCOVERED BEACHES IN THE CARIBBEAN? DREAM ON.

Still, it's surprising how low-key the tourism is on tiny, sparsely populated Barbuda. Though it rhymes with Bermuda and begins with the same letters as Barbados, Barbuda is quite different from those popular Caribbean destinations, a hard-to-reach backwater in the Lesser Antilles. Seen from above, it's a mere dot in the ocean compared with its sister island, Antigua ㉙, 48km (30 miles) due north. Most of its 1,200 inhabitants live in one village—the island's only village, in fact—named Codrington after the British family that leased Barbuda as a plantation for much of the colonial era. The landscape tends to be flat, arid, and scrubby, and most roads are unpaved. You can count the lodgings options on one hand, though among them are two of the Caribbean's most exclusive small resorts, Coco Point Lodge and the K-Club.

Barbuda.

Yet small as it is, Barbuda has some of the most breathtaking beaches in the entire Caribbean—27km (17 miles) of rosy pink-sand beaches and sugary white-sand beaches, all lapped by gentle, azure seas and protected by barrier reefs. (Ships that foundered on those same reefs add to the island's diving attractions.) Beaches on the southwestern shore, facing the Caribbean Sea, are best for swimming, including picture-perfect **Pink Sand Beach,** which owes its blushing pink hues to crushed coral, an effect that's especially picturesque at sunset. Beaches such as **Hog Bay** and **Rubbish Bay** on the island's eastern shore, fronting the slightly rougher waters of the Atlantic, are better for strolling and shell collecting.

If you want to see more of the island beyond the beaches, you can rent a four-wheel-drive or have a taxi driver give you a tour. In the 18th century, the island served as a breadbasket for the workers on Antigua's sugar plantations and also supplied slave labor to work the sugar cane fields (all slaves were freed in 1834). The Codrington family remains a ghostly presence on the island: The ruins of their 18th-century estate manor, **Highland House,** are located on the highest point on the island. Other places to visit include the **Frigate Bird Sanctuary,** located in the huge north-western lagoon. Accessible only by boat, the sanctuary is the Caribbean's largest, home to some 5,000 frigate birds as well as individuals from another 170 bird species, including pelicans, herons, and tropical mockingbirds. Even in high season, there are more birds than people on Barbuda—how many Caribbean islands can boast that kind of ratio?

ⓘ www.antigua-barbuda.org.

✈ Barbuda (15-min. flight from Antigua).

🚂 **Barbuda Express** (ℂ **268/560-7989;** www.antiguaferries.com) 90 min.

🛏 $$$ **Coco Point Lodge, Coco Point.** (ℂ **268/462-3816;** www.cocopoint.com). $$$ **Lighthouse Bay Resort** (ℂ **888/214-8552;** www.lighthousebayresort.com).

78 **Escape the Crowd**

Shi Shi Beach
Where Eagles Soar
Washington State, U.S.A.

IF YOU'RE REALLY HARD-CORE, YOU COULD DO THE 5-DAY HIKE UP THE rugged Olympic coast from rocky Rialto Beach, staying overnight at various national park campgrounds along the way. Or you can drive down from Neah Bay to the trailhead, which leaves you with only a 2-mile (3.2km) hike through spruce forest and bog across a corner of the Makah Indian Reservation. (**Warning:** The last 150-yard descent down the bluff is incredibly steep—especially the return.) Either way, an excursion to Shi Shi Beach is a bracing adventure, with bald eagles circling overhead and deer and raccoons lurking in the woods at beach edge.

Located in the extreme northwestern corner of Washington state, Olympic National Park is a land of impenetrable, rain-soaked forests and steep, glacier-carved mountains. Most people can summon up a mental image of its centerpiece, majestic snow-capped Mount Olympus. Northwest hikers, however, know that some 73 miles (117km) of coastline have also been preserved as part of the national park—and its most spectacular beaches can be reached only on foot.

Shi Shi Beach.

Of those beaches, Shi Shi Beach is probably the most spectacular, stretching for 2 miles (3.2km) along the majestic curve of **Makah Bay.** Shi Shi was a late addition to the park, annexed only in 1976—a move intended to prevent land developers from siting beach homes here. (Before then, it had been a hippie hangout.) Thanks to a Travel Channel report touting Shi Shi as one of the country's most beautiful beaches, it's no secret anymore, and you're likely to encounter other campers and hikers in summer. But the sort of people who come here tend to respect its wilderness vibe, and Shi Shi still feels unspoiled, with no facilities beyond a couple of pit toilets.

Shi Shi isn't a swimming beach—this is the Northwest after all, and the waters are too cold, the pounding surf too risky—but it's a brilliant place to stroll, especially at low tide, contemplating the sheltering dunes and bluffs, the seal-covered offshore rocks, the trailing wisps of fog. South of Petroleum Creek you can begin to glimpse **Point of the Arches,** a 1 mile-long (1.6km) conglomeration of sea stacks and natural arches that runs down the coast. Collect an armful of driftwood and build a campfire on the beach; better yet, camp overnight (obtain a camping permit from the Wilderness Information Center in Port Angeles) so you can enjoy Shi Shi's sunset views—the sort of sunset views that the word "awesome" was invented to describe.

ⓘ www.nps.gov/olym.

✈ Seattle/Tacoma (224 miles/360km) or Port Angeles (93 miles/ 150km).

🚢 Washington State Ferries (ⓒ **888/808-7977;** www.wsdot. wa.gov/ferries) from Seattle to Bainbridge Island, Bremerton, or Kingston.

🛏 $$ **Ocean Park Resort at La Push,** 330 Ocean Dr., La Push (ⓒ **800/487-1267** or 360/374-5267; www.ocean-park.org). $ **Olympic Suites Inn,** 800 Olympic Dr., Forks (ⓒ **800/262-3433** or 360/374-5400; www.olympicsuitesinn.com).

Molera State Park
Beachcombing in Big Sur
Big Sur, California, U.S.A.

DRIVING UP THE BIG SUR COAST ON WINDING, SCENIC HIGHWAY 1 IS already an exercise in getting away from it all. Having traced the spectacular California coastline for miles, you're suddenly plunged into a mysterious forest of majestic dark conifers, often shrouded in fog. (Don't wait for a sunny day—Big Sur *belongs* in fog.) With the heavy L.A.-to-San Francisco traffic all inland on U.S. 101 or I-5, the road seems suddenly empty, with few buildings of any sort, not even gas stations. Yet every once in awhile the trees part and amazing ocean vistas take your breath away, overlooking craggy bluffs to glinting Pacific horizons.

Down those bluffs lie a number of beautiful isolated sand beaches—the only catch is, you'll have to hike to most of them. But really, that's a good thing. The one large beach easily accessible by car, **Sand Dollar Beach** (off of Hwy. 1 near Gorda) quickly fills up with surfers and college kids on a summer day; even wide golden **Pfeiffer Beach** (Sycamore Canyon Rd., just south of Pfeiffer-Big Sur State Park) gets its share of beachgoers. But Andrew Molera State Park (about 3 miles/5km south of the Point Sur lighthouse) rarely gets crowds on its stunning sandy beach, 2½ miles (4km) long and handily sheltered from coastal winds by a large bluff. Casual beachgoers may be deterred by the 1-mile (1.6km) hike required to reach the beach, but that's their problem: The **Creamery Meadow Trail** (so called because this used to be a dairy farm) is a wide, scenic path through wildflower meadows and stands of sycamore trees, with great mountain views to enjoy en route. You basically follow the Big Sur River down to the sea; at the end, you may have to ford the river to reach the beach, so bring water shoes.

The dramatic bluffs of Big Sur, California.

Molera State Park is popular with campers and hikers; if you plan to camp overnight, show up before noon to grab a campsite. Because campsites are limited, however—and many campers are off hiking instead of beachcombing—the beach is never too crowded. While the water is too cold and rough for serious swimming, you could spend hours here collecting driftwood, exploring tide pools, and climbing around the rocks. To make your Big Sur expedition even more memorable, sign up for a gallop along the beach with **Molera Big Sur Trail Rides** (✆ **831/625-5486;** www.molerahorsebacktours.com), which offers various hour-long outings daily April to December.

There are usually a few surfers out riding the beach's modest waves; no doubt you'll also encounter a few countercultural beach bums. Beatnik novelist Jack Kerouac once wrote a whole book about escaping to Big Sur—now you'll understand why.

ⓘ www.bigsurcalifornia.com.

✈ San Francisco International (140 miles/225km).

🛏 $ **Andrew Molera State Park** (✆ **831/667-2315;** www.parks.ca.gov). $ **Big Sur Lodge,** 47225 Hwy. 1 (✆ **800/424-4787** or 831/667-3100; www.bigsurlodge.com).

Escape the Crowd 80

Los Roques
An Island to Yourself
Venezuela

IT'S NOT AS IF NO TOURISTS KNOW ABOUT LOS ROQUES. AS SOON AS you get off the plane at the Caracas airport, you'll see tour operators advertising day trips to this national marine park, about 166km (103 miles) north along the coast. Yet once you arrive—the archipelago's only town, Gran Roque, is a quick hour's flight from Caracas—all visitors disperse quickly, taking catamarans off to any of hundreds of tiny uninhabited islands and cays with wind-ruffled white beaches and marvelous coral reefs, where you and your companions are left alone to dive, swim, kayak, or fish to your heart's delight. Warm, crystal-clear waters beckon, in various alluring shades of blue. It's entirely feasible to do it as a day trip, but why leave so soon? Book a room in one of the park's several small posadas (book *way* in advance) so you can wake up next morning and do it all over again.

Declared a national park in 1972, Los Roques—the name means simply "the rocks"—protects vast areas of sea-grass beds, mangroves, and coral reef, the largest marine park in the Caribbean. It's an important sea-turtle nesting ground and an international Ramsar site, with 92 recorded bird species including brown- and red-footed boobies, pelicans, gulls, terns, and even a few pink flamingos. Before tourism entered the picture, Gran Roque was a fishing town, with the main catch being lobster. Tourism drives the economy nowadays, but the government has deliberately kept it low-key—no mega-resorts or nightlife zones. Four crushed-coral-and-sand streets run lengthwise through the town of Gran Roque, but there's not much traffic to carry, just a garbage truck, a water truck, and a handful of golf carts.

Healthy barrier reefs surround the archipelago, making it a premier dive spot; sheer walls on the southern and eastern flanks drop off steeply to depths of as much as 900m (2,952 ft.). With 61 different kinds of coral and some 280 fish species, there's always something to see underwater. Flat waters and near-constant trade winds from the northeast make for fantastic sailing, windsurfing, and kitesurfing. Anglers stalk bonefish *(pez ratón)* in shallow waters and grass flats all over the archipelago.

But the most popular activity here is a lot less strenuous—a regimen of getting dropped off on an isolated little island in the morning with a beach umbrella, some chaise longues, and a cooler full of food and drink, and getting picked up again in the late afternoon. Hmmm—have we got any takers?

ⓘ www.los-roques.com.

✈ Gran Roque.

🛏 $$ **Posada Acquamarina,** Calle Principal #148, Gran Roque (📞 **58/412/310-1962;** www.posada-acquamarina.com). $$ **Posada Acuarela,** The Playground #117, Gran Roque (📞 **58/212/953-6455** or 58/237/221-1228 or; www.posadaacuarela.com).

Half Moon Bay
Rum-Runners & Sandpipers
California, U.S.A.

UNDER COVER OF NIGHT, THE LITTLE BOATS WOULD SLIP INTO FOGGY Half Moon Bay, scooting around offshore rocks to find a calm open beach. The crates and barrels they unloaded in the darkness were slung in the trunks of 1920s-era roadsters and rushed to local roadhouses and inns, where a nod to the waiter could still get you a slug of rum or whiskey, despite Prohibition.

Today, Half Moon Bay is more for daytime beachgoers than nighttime run-runners. The last scenic gasp on the coastal drive up from Los Angeles, this sheltered crescent of Pacific coastline (hence the name) lies only 25 miles (40km) south of San Francisco. Half Moon Bay's gently sloping golden beaches are backed not by rounded dunes but by jagged low cliffs topped with flowery scrub. The shore's abundant bird life includes sandpipers, pelicans, shearwaters, herons, red-tailed hawks, and the endangered Western snowy plover, a brown-and-white shore bird so tiny it can shelter from the wind in a human footprint left in the sand.

Blessed by a mild climate with lots of sea breezes (morning fogs burn off by noon), Half Moon Bay is one of the gentler swimming options on the northern California coast. And it certainly has a full complement of beaches. Right along Highway 1 (here called Cabrillo Hwy.) by the town of Half Moon Bay, Half Moon Bay State Beach runs for 4 miles (6km), a series of beaches connected by a 3-mile (5km) blufftop jogging and bike trail, buffered by farmland from the town. (There's no tacky beachside strip of souvenir shops and crab shacks.) From north to south, they are **Dunes Beach** (at the end of Young Avenue), **Venice Beach** (at Venice Boulevard), and broad **Francis Beach** (at Kelly Ave.), which has camping facilities. South of town lie several other state beaches, including **Poplar State Beach** (at Poplar Avenue), the only beach that allows dogs and horses; a secluded pocket beach at **Cowells Ranch,** with rocks full of basking harbor seals; **San Gregorio State Beach,** a barrier beach at the mouth of San Gregorio Creek; and bluff-protected **Pomponio State Beach,** which has a small lagoon full of wading birds and is close to the bird refuge of **Pescadero Marsh.**

With so many choices, beachgoers can pick their action, whether it's sandcastle building, beach volleyball, bird-watching, or poking around rock pools for tidal creatures. Whale-watching expeditions to see humpback whales and migrating gray whales depart year-round from the enclosed cove of Pillar Point Harbor, at the bay's north end. A couple miles offshore from Pillar Point, big-wave surfers head to the Mavericks surf area, where the waves are sometimes over 80 ft. (24m) high—not for amateurs!

ⓘ www.parks.ca.gov.

✈ San Francisco International.

🛏 $$ **Best Western Half Moon Bay Lodge,** 2400 Cabrillo Hwy. S., Half Moon Bay (𝒸 **650/726-9000;** www.halfmoonbay lodge.com). $ **Coastside Inn,** 230 S. Cabrillo Hwy., Half Moon Bay (𝒸 **650/726-3400;** www.coastsideinn.com).

82 Wildlife

Assateague Island National Seashore
Doing the Pony on the Eastern Shore
Maryland & Virginia, U.S.A.

THANKS TO THE CHILDREN'S BOOK *MISTY OF CHINCOTEAGUE,* LOTS OF kids dream of visiting Assateague Island, home to a native herd of shaggy wild ponies. Legend claims they descended from horses that swam ashore from a shipwrecked Spanish galleon centuries ago, though the truth is more prosaic—more likely they were put there in the late 1600s by English settlers who found the island a natural corral. Confusingly, they're called Chincoteague ponies, since residents of that neighboring island regularly round them up to cull the herd. Assateague itself, however, is uninhabited, a wind-ruffled, marshy 37-mile-long (60km) barrier island that offers nothing but wildlife refuges, weather-beaten charm, and one long sandy strip of glorious white Atlantic seacoast.

Wind, waves, and storms continually remake this fragile outpost on the Eastern Shore; every year the island moves closer to the mainland, as its oceanward beaches erode and sediment fills in the landward shore. If it hadn't been for a huge nor'easter in 1962, Assateague might have become a resort development; after that storm leveled the island, plans changed and in 1965 Assateague became a National Seashore.

A causeway connects Chincoteague to the mainland, and another causeway leads on to Assateague. A strict quota system controls the number of cars on Assateague at any one time. To get to the beach, it's a good idea to take one of the narrated bus tours that run along a paved 4½-mile (7.2km) Wildlife Drive through the marshes of **Assateague's Chincoteague Wildlife Refuge.** You can also walk or cycle along the road, but you can't drive your own car until after 3pm. At the end of the main road, you pass shifting white dunes and come to the **Assateague National Seashore,** a pristine beach with bathhouses, lifeguards, and a visitor center. It's a great place for clamming, seashell collecting, surf fishing, beach hiking, and swimming—or maybe just settling on the sand, feeling the salt spray in your face, and imagining the ghost of a wrecked Spanish galleon.

Visitors to Assateague Island can also enjoy some excellent bird watching—it's a prime Atlantic flyway habitat where peregrine falcons, snow geese, great blue heron, and snowy egrets have been sighted. Dolphins swim off shore; bald eagles soar overhead. There are ranger-guided programs available from both the Maryland Barrier Island Visitor Center (✆ **410/641-1441**) and the Virginia Toms Cove Visitor Center (✆ **757/336-6577**). As for the horses, they roam freely in the saltmarshes of the Maryland

Though it's famous for its ponies, Assateague Island is also a first-rate spot for bird-watching.

section of the park; in the Virginia section, look for them in the marshes along Beach Road and from the observation platform on the Woodland Trail. Keep your distance, though—they are wild creatures, after all.

ⓘ Assateague Island National Seashore (ℂ **410/ 641-1441;** www. nps.gov/asis).

✈ Norfolk VA.

🛏 $$$ **Island Motor Inn Resort,** 4391 N. Main St., Chincoteague (ℂ **757/336-3141;** www.islandmotorinn.com). $$ **Refuge Inn,** 7058 Maddox Blvd., Chincoteague (ℂ **888/257-0038** or 757/336-5511; www.refugeinn.com).

Padre Island National Seashore
Sun & Surf, Texas-Style
Texas, U.S.A.

EVERYTHING'S BIGGER IN THE LONE STAR STATE, AND PADRE ISLAND is a stellar example: It's the longest section of undeveloped barrier island in the world. A narrow strip of land lying between the Gulf of Mexico and the shallow hypersaline Laguna Madre lagoon, **Padre Island National Seashore** unspools for 70 miles (113km) of sand, low dunes, and rippling prairie grasses.

Connected by bridge to the mainland, Padre Island is divided by hairline channels from Mustang Island State Beach to the north and South Padre Island to the south, known for its cheap hotels and raucous bar scene. On North Padre Island, however, wildlife takes over from the wild life. For such a narrow strip of land—it's barely a mile wide—Padre Island teems with wildlife. Coyotes, badgers, raccoons, opossums, rats, squirrels, and bats populate the low wildflower-studded grasslands. Positioned right on the Central Flyway, a major bird migration route, it's a bird-watcher's heaven. As many as 350 species have been recorded here, either wintering in its temperate climate or stopping to breed and nest in the tidal flats and marshes on their way to more northerly climes. It's also an area of rich sea life, including four different species of sea turtle—in summer you may be lucky enough to witness the Park Service's hatchling release program of rare Kemp's Ridley turtles. Check out the park ranger's calendar to see what beach walks, campfire programs, and bird-watching outings are scheduled during your visit.

Although it's under the jurisdiction of the National Park Service, don't expect a *totally* pristine encounter with nature here: Vehicles are allowed to drive right on the beach in most places (a Texas tradition), and given the seashore's proximity to Corpus Christi and Houston, you'll most likely contend with convoys of SUVs on weekends and holidays and whenever the weather's nice. Furthermore, plenty of flotsam from the Gulf of Mexico makes its way to the

Padre Island National Seashore is a bird-watcher's heaven.

shores of Padre Island; beachcombers can find plenty of shells and driftwood, but there's also a lot of metal, glass, and plastic washing up on shore. Nevertheless, it's a great swimming environment; the warm salty water on both sides of the island gives everything that floats in it extra buoyancy. The half-mile beach at the lagoon's Bird Island is also a great windsurfing site.

At the northern end of the seashore, **Malaquite Beach** is the most unspoiled beach in the area—it's closed to vehicular traffic— with simple wood-frame picnic shelters where you can set up for a day of shore exploration.

(i) Malaquite Visitors Center, Milepost O, Park Road 22 (Hwy. 358) (© **361/949-8068;** www.nps.gov/pais).

✈ Corpus Christi International.

⇌ $$ **Hawthorn Suites by Wyndham,** 15201 Windward Dr., Corpus Christi (© **361/949-2400;** www.wyndham.com). $ Camping permits available at park visitor center.

Wildlife 84

Seven Mile Beach
Stingray City
Grand Cayman, the Cayman Islands

IT ALL BEGAN IN THE 1980S, WHEN FISHERMEN JUST OFFSHORE OF Grand Cayman Island cleaned their catch every evening in the shallow, sunny waters of North Sound, just off the island's northwestern tip. Over the years, stingrays began to swarm in to feast on the scraps, like a pack of dogs waiting to be fed. And while they still come in droves, these days the fishermen have been replaced by snorkelers and divers, who allow these giant, gentle creatures to suck up bait up from their flat, open hands. The animals swim right over your shoulders, as tame as any wild animal could be; petting them is like stroking some wondrous newfangled silk-and-velvet fabric.

Known for its clear, warm waters, Grand Cayman—the largest and most populated of the three Cayman Islands, a British crown colony—is one of the best diving destinations in the world, with more than 200 named and explored sites. Most visitors also spend at least part of their time snorkeling at Parrot's Reef or Smith's Cove, south of George Town, lush reefs abounding with parrotfish, coral, sea fans, and sponges. There are many reputable dive shops here (try Don Foster's Dive Cayman, www.donfosters.com; or Seven Mile Watersports, www.7milediver.com) and all of them offer Stingray City stops on their dive tours.

But Grand Cayman has another ace to offer visitors: one of the Caribbean's most stunning beaches, Seven Mile Beach. Lying just north of the capital, George Town, Seven Mile Beach follows the long lazy curve of West Bay at the western end of the island. It's actually only 8.9km (5½) miles long, but no one's got their measuring tapes out. That wide expanse of powdery white sand lined with silver thatch palms always seems to have room for everyone, even at the height of the winter tourist season.

. While there are several other smaller beaches around the island, most of Grand Cayman's hotels, restaurants, shops, and dive shops are located along Seven-Mile Beach. The sand here is noticeably clean and litter-free, with almost no peddlers hawking their wares (in contrast to that other Seven-Mile beauty in Negril, Jamaica 🔵**48**). If a morning or sunset gallop along the beach sounds like your style, contact **Horse Back in Paradise with Nicki** (www.cayman horseriding.com).

Bird-lovers may also want to take an excursion over to **Little Cayman Island,** where a colony of more than 5,000 pairs of red-footed boobies nest every February in the saltwater lagoon of **Booby Pond Nature Reserve** (www.nationaltrust.org.ky/info/boobypond.html). Every winter night at twilight, a dramatic battle for survival is played out between frigate birds and the boobies; it's a memorable nature spectacle to behold.

ⓘ Tourist office (✆ **345/949-0623;** www.caymanislands.ky).

✈ Grand Cayman.

🛏 $$ **The Anchorage,** Seven Mile Beach (✆ **813/333-6532** from the U.S. or 345/945-4088; www.theanchoragecayman.com). $$ **Silver Sands Condominiums,** West Bay Rd., Seven Mile Beach (✆ **345/949-3343;** www.silversandscondos.com).

Point Reyes National Seashore
The White Cliffs of Marin
Northern California, U.S.A.

WHEN SIR FRANCIS DRAKE AND HIS GLOBE-CIRCLING CREW HAULED the *Golden Hinde* onto this sweeping beach in 1579, one look at its bleached limestone bluffs made them homesick for the white cliffs of Dover.

What Drake didn't know was that this starkly beautiful peninsula is a geological freak, a chunk of continent transported some 300 miles (483km) north by the San Andreas Fault. It's a windswept and rough-hewn landscape, where rocky headlands tumble down to a textured plain of coastal scrub threaded with estuaries, meandering creeks, and still lagoons; in the interior, moss-cloaked Douglas firs and California redwoods thickly cover Inverness Ridge.

Point Reyes is a birding hotspot, with 490 bird species recorded—nearly half of all North American birds—the highest avian diversity of any national park. Its boulder-strewn shoreline is also home to four species of pinnipeds: harbor seals, California sea lions, Steller sea lions, and a booming winter population of the once-rare Northern elephant seal. From January through April, beachcombers regularly spot mother gray whales cruising with their calves along the shoreline.

With some 80 miles (130km) of rugged shoreline, Point Reyes has several wide sand beaches, which among California's cleanest. Take your pick—you can dabble in the sheltered waters along the curve of **Drake's Bay,** below the lighthouse point, or get your pulse racing on the surf-pounded **Pacific Ocean front,** which breasts the sea for nearly 10 miles (16km) north of the lighthouse. Swimmers beware—you'll need a wetsuit in these cold waters, and be vigilant about rip tides and sneaker waves. Kayakers generally stick to the calmer waters of **Tomales Bay,** the narrow inlet that divides Point Reyes from the mainland; ocean kayaking is risky around here.

The Point Reyes seashore is only half an hour's drive north of Stinson Beach **47**, but it's a different experience entirely—much more of a wild and lonely place, where you can slow down and take the pulse of nature. None of these beaches ever get crowded, but the most-visited strands are probably **Drakes Beach** and **Limantour Beach,** both on the bay, and the **Great Beach** that faces the Pacific. These can all be easily accessed from the North and South Beach parking lots; the rest of the park's shoreline requires an overland hike. If you're interested in tidepooling, follow the Coast Trail down the bay to **Sculptured Beach,** or, near Bolinas Point at the south end of the bay, **Palomarin Beach,** which is close to the Point Reyes Bird Observatory. Nature-lovers may also seek out the ocean beach at **Abbotts Lagoon,** a 1½-mile (2.5km) hike off Pierce Point Road—a serene habitat for migrating shorebirds in the fall and ducks in winter, where snowy plovers nest in the dunes every summer.

(i) Point Reyes National Seashore, 1 Bear Valley Rd., Point Reyes Station (© **415/464-5100;** www.nps.gov/pore).

✈ San Francisco/Oakland (39 miles/63km).

🛏 $ **Point Reyes Hostel,** Point Reyes National Seashore (© **415/663-8811;** http://norcalhostels.org/reyes). $$ **Abalone Inn,** 12355 Sir Francis Drake Blvd., Inverness Park (© **877/416-0458** or 415/663-9149; www.abaloneinn.com).

86 Wildlife

Canaveral National Seashore
Open Space on the Space Coast
New Smyrna, Florida, U.S.A.

AT THE DAWN OF THE SPACE RACE, IN 1958, THIS SLEEPY SECTION OF Florida's east coast seemed ideal for launching rockets: It was relatively close to the equator's rotation, far from the urban clutter of Jacksonville and Miami, and open to the Atlantic Ocean. NASA snapped up as much land as it could, and Cape Canaveral's space center—renamed Kennedy Space Center in 1963—was launched.

As it turned out, NASA overdid the land grab. Still, anxious to prevent development from creeping too close to its launch pads, NASA turned its extra acreage to good use: In 1975 it gave the National Park Service a 24-mile-long (39km) barrier island just north of the space facility, along with the bird-filled marshes and lagoon behind it, creating the Canaveral National Seashore.

Considering what a tourist attraction the Kennedy Space Center has become, it's a blessing for wildlife that that coastline was protected. The Space Coast, as this now-busy area has been dubbed, has 72 miles (116km) of beaches, but this is its most unspoiled section by far. Backed by silvery dunes, cabbage palms, sea grapes, and palmettos, the barrier beach is divided into three sections—northernmost **Apollo** (named after the rocket program), where the visitor center is located; **Klondike,** reachable only by hiking (back country permit required); and beautiful **Playalinda,** accessed from the south via Florida 402. (Expect to encounter nude sunbathers on Playalinda's more deserted stretches.) On the way to Playalinda, you'll pass the entrance to **Merritt Island National Wildlife Refuge** (www.nbbd.com/godo/minwr); it's a worthwhile detour, where you can drive the self-guided 6-mile-long (10km) **Black Point Wildlife Drive,** which identifies natural features in a tranquil preserve of marshes and coastal hammocks.

Beachgoers who choose Canaveral over other area strands, like lively Jetty Park in Port Canaveral or the surfer-friendly Cocoa Beach Pier, generally prefer a more back-to-nature experience. There are no picnic tables or snack bars here; restrooms, parking lots, and boardwalk paths is about the extent of the amenities. And those other beaches don't have walking trails where you can spot herons, pelicans, reddish egrets, wood storks, Florida scrub jays, and dolphins and manatees around Mosquito Lagoon; there's also a marked canoe trail through the intracoastal marshes of Shipyard Island. Don't miss the heady sea views from atop 35-ft.-tall (11m) **Turtle Mound,** built centuries ago by Native Americans entirely of oyster shells. Along the beach, all major species of sea turtles nest in summer, while ruddy turnstones, willets, and sanderlings explore the waterline in winter.

In July 2011, an era ended when the last space shuttle took off from Cape Canaveral; no longer will the neighboring seashore have to shut down for launch days. NASA may have transformed the Space Coast, but the wildlife outlasted the rocket ships—which is good news for everyone.

ⓘ Canaveral National Seashore visitor center, 7611 S. Atlantic Ave., New Smyrna Beach (℗ **321/267-1110;** www.nps.gov/cana).

✈ Melbourne International/Orlando International (70 miles/ 113km).

⇌ $$ **Riverview Hotel,** 103 Flagler Ave., New Smyrna Beach (℗ **800/945-7416** or 386/428-5858; www.riverviewhotel.com). $$ **DoubleTree Cocoa Beach Oceanfront,** 2080 N. Atlantic Ave., Cocoa Beach (℗ **321/783-9222;** www.cocoabeachdoubletree. com).

87 Wildlife

Ship Island
Playing Gulf
Mississippi, U.S.A.

AT THE EASTERN END OF THE GULF ISLANDS NATIONAL SEASHORE, Florida's barrier islands—like Santa Rosa Island ㊾—lie close to the mainland, tethered by highway bridges. The Mississippi half of the park is another matter altogether. Its five islands seem almost stranded in the Gulf of Mexico, 11 miles (18km) across the shallow Mississippi Sound from Gulfport and Biloxi. Most of them can only be accessed by private boat, which is great for preserving their natural wildness—but not so great for human visitors. What's a Delta beachgoer to do?

The answer is simple: **West Ship Island.** This skinny crescent of land has the only deep-water harbor between Mobile Bay and the Mississippi River, big enough for ferries to dock. You can take a half- or a full-day boat trip out of Gulfport, run by **Ship Island Excursions** (© **866/466-7386** or 228/864-1014; www.mssshipisland.com). Chugging across the sound, you'll get an extra treat: Atlantic bottlenose dolphins merrily swimming alongside the boat, like Ship Island's unofficial greeters.

Remote and undeveloped, flat scrubby Ship Island lies at the mercies of the Gulf of Mexico. In 1969 Hurricane Camille sliced the island in two, creating East and West Ship Islands; Hurricane Katrina knocked down the lighthouse in 2005. In 2008, Hurricane Ike nearly submerged both East and West Ship Island. But such storms are natural for a barrier island; while they may raze human-built structures, they also tend to sweep clear sandy beaches, making them prime open habitat for certain shore birds like least terns and black skimmers.

Unfortunately, the shore birds weren't prepared for the Deep-water oil rig's explosion in March 2010, which sent oil gushing for months into the western Gulf. Tar balls washed up on beaches, oil oozed into coastal marshes, and waterbirds were unable to fly with their oil-coated feathers. Rescue efforts at Ship Island proved critical to the Gulf shores' slow recovery; the beaches are open again and ready to welcome visitors.

Park rangers meet ferries at the dock, offering tours of the park's top historic site: Civil-War-era **Fort Massachusetts,** a circular brick fort on the western tip that was used as a base for attacks on nearby New Orleans and Mobile. From the fort, follow a boardwalk across the islands to the south beach, fronting the Gulf of Mexico, where most visitors swim. Lifeguards are on duty in summer; beach chairs and umbrellas are available for rent (there's little shade on this treeless island). Swimming is popular in these warm waters; so are snorkeling and boogie-boarding, though you'll have to bring your own gear across on the ferry. Compared to the condo-lined beaches of Biloxi and Gulfport, Ship Island's pillowy white sands are relaxed and uncrowded—good news for the plovers and sandpipers, too.

(i) (✆) **850/934-2600** or 228/875-9057, extension 100; www.nps. gov/guis.

✈ Gulfport-Biloxi International Airport.

🛏 $$$ **Courtyard by Marriott Gulfport Beachfront,** 1600 E. Beach Blvd., Gulfport ((✆) **800/442-0887** or 228/864-4310; www. marriott.com). $$ **Holiday Inn Gulfport/Airport,** 9515 Hwy. 49, Gulfport ((✆) **888/465-4329** or 228/679-1700; www.ichotelsgroup. com).

88 Wildlife

Fernando do Noronha
Protecting Paradise
Brazil

WHEN EXPLORER AMERIGO VESPUCCI FIRST LANDED UPON THIS REMOTE Brazilian island in 1504, he delivered a simple verdict: "Here is paradise." Luckily, the Brazilian government has done all the right things to keep it like paradise.

The largest of 21 islands on the Brazilian archipelago of the same name, Fernando de Noronha owes much of its eco-purity to its remote location, approximately 483km (300 miles) off Brazil's northeast coast. It's so remote, in fact, that until the late 1980s it served as a military base and prison. But considering the island's stellar natural attractions—dazzling beaches, diamond-clear waters bathed by warm African currents, mossy volcanic hills—it could easily have become overrun with resorts and cruise visitors. Instead, thanks to a highly responsible conservation ethos—70% of the archipelago is national parkland, Brazil's first national marine park—development is rigidly controlled. The government allows only 460 nonresidents on the island at one time.

What's at stake isn't just lovely landscape, but an undersea world teeming with sea turtles, clownfish, parrotfish, lemon sharks and reef sharks, rays of all types (mantas are not uncommon), and

167

Spinner dolphins in Fernando do Noronha

especially its large population of resident dolphins—spinner dolphins, so named for the exuberant spin they do as they leap out of the water. The Baia dos Golfinhos, where some 600 dolphins live and breed, has a perfectly lovely 2.3km (1½-mile) crescent of sand, but it's strictly off-limits to visitors—although you can watch the dolphins from a cliff overlooking the beach (binoculars help).

Only 100 people per day are allowed to visit the **Praia de Atalaia** beach, where snorkeling is permitted in the shallow tidal pools for only 25 minutes—with no suntan lotion, please. Strict controls are also exercised during turtle-hatching season at **Praia do Leão** (named for the rock offshore that resembles a sea lion), a critical nesting site for turtles. Other fantastic beaches for swimming and snorkeling include **Baía do Sueste,** a pretty crescent beach with calm shallow waters; and beautiful **Baía do Sancho,** with its red-tinged sand and crystal-clear blue water set below sheer red cliffs (you climb down via iron ladders). Lodging on the island is mostly in small pousadas rather than big resorts, so you're encouraged to explore the whole island, tooling in dune buggies around the scrubby interior's red dirt roads.

December and January are favored months for surfers; July through October is prime diving season, when Fernando de Noronha offers warm waters with incredible visibility. Divers must use one of three approved operators—no one's taking any chances with this paradise.

ⓘ www.noronha.pe.gov.br.

✈ Fernando de Noronha (1 hr., 40 min. from Recife; 1 hr., 10 min. from Natal).

🛏 $$$ **Pousada Maravilha,** Vila do Sueste. (ⓒ **55/81/3619-0028;** www.pousadamaravilha.com.br). $$ **Pousada Solar dos Ventos,** Vila do Sueste. (ⓒ **55/81/3619-1347;** www.pousada solardosventos.com.br).

89 Wildlife

Shark Bay
Dolphins & Dugongs & Sharks, Oh My!
Northwest Cape, Western Australia

SHARK BAY—HOW MUCH MORE ADVENTUROUS COULD A PLACE sound? But the truth is, most visitors come here not to see blood-thirsty sharks but to ooh and aah over the bottlenose dolphins that cruise every morning into the shallow water of a former pearling camp known as **Monkey Mia.** (And no, there are no monkeys here either.) Rangers instruct visitors to stand still in the knee-deep water while the dolphins glide past; you're not allowed to pet them, but they playfully nudge the tourists from time to time.

The dolphins have been coming reliably for some 40 years now to this protected bay with its tranquil blue waters and clean white beaches. The Monkey Mia Resort is also a laidback resort, located right on palm-fringed **Dolphin Beach,** where you can swim, sail, snorkel, or even take a beach camel ride when the dolphins aren't stealing the show.

While Western Australia is somewhat off the usual circuit for North American travelers, the rewards for coming here are near-constant blue skies, no tourist crowds (compared to the Great Barrier Reef), and great access to wildlife. A 2½-hour cruise on the sailing catamaran Shotover (© **61/8/99 481 481;** www.monkeymia wildsights.com.au), leaving from the Monkey Mia resort, will show you waters heaving with fish, manta rays, sea turtles, sea snakes, and either migrating humpback whales (June–Oct) or the world's largest population of dugongs, aka manatees (Sept–Apr), attracted by—no coincidence—the world's largest seagrass meadows.

On the harsh **Peron Peninsula,** which juts out into Shark Bay, hiking trails in **Francois Peron National Park** offer sweeping sea views from dunes and dramatic red coastal cliffs. Nature takes some bizarre shapes around here. At **Shell Beach,** 45km (27 miles) southeast of Denham, what looks like white sand turns out to be billions of tiny white seashells. To the southeast, the **Hamelin Pool Marine Nature Reserve** is a hypersaline pond full of weirdly lumpy foot-high fossil formations called stromatolites.

So where are the sharks? Up on the Northwest Cape, a day's drive north on Highway 1. At Exmouth, tour boats take people out to snorkel with gentle whale sharks, the world's largest fish (true whales are bigger, but they're mammals), from late March—June. November through late February, nighttime turtle-watch tours witness green and loggerhead turtles nesting on the cape's beaches. Any time of year, diving is excellent on the Cape's Ningaloo Reef, which offers 250 species of coral and 450 kinds of fish to marvel at—grouper, manta rays, octopus, morays, potato cod, false killer whales, and, (naturally) sharks.

ⓘ Monkey Mia visitor center (© **61/8/9948 1366;** www.sharkbay. asn.au).

✈ Shark Bay or Exmouth.

🛏 $–$$$ **Monkey Mia Dolphin Resort,** Monkey Mia Rd. (© **61/8/9948 1320;** www.monkeymia.com.au).

Kiawah Island
Playing in the Rough
South Carolina, U.S.A.

TO MANY MODERN RESORTGOERS, KIAWAH ISLAND IS SYNONYMOUS with golf—there are five world-class golf courses on this low-lying sea island, their velvety sculpted fairways winding around patches of maritime forest and rustling saltmarsh, rolling past the dunes and steely surf of Kiawah's Atlantic beachfront. But how many golf resorts have a full-time crew of nature preserve rangers?

Connected by bridge to the mainland, and conveniently close to Charleston, Kiawah was for many years an indigo plantation and cattle farm. When resort development first began on Kiawah in the 1970s (the entire island is one high-toned property, comprised of a main hotel and several residential villas), its forward-thinking owners declared their commitment to conservation and eco-sensitivity. Alongside the golf courses, Kiawah has laid out some 30 miles (48km) of biking and hiking trails that weave through pristine marshland; more than 100 acres (40 hectares) of the resort is protected parkland and bird sanctuaries. (Visit the Nature Center at Night Heron Park for wildlife tours and programs.) Much of the island is still wild and untamed, with local ecosystems preserved in a tangled forest of pines, sand palms, and sea myrtle. Roads are lined with native live oaks draped in Spanish moss. The golden marsh grasses provide cover for wading birds, alligators, and the occasional manatee, while shimmering saltwater tidal creeks hold sweet shrimp, crabs, and fish—you may even spot a bottlenose dolphin or two if you're kayaking around the creeks or the Kiawah River.

And then there's the beach, a wide swath of soft white, pillowy sand that fringes 17 miles (27km) of southern Atlantic coast. Sparkling surf and surprisingly warm waters make it a great swimming beach, with just enough wave action for a little boogie-boarding.

There's even wildlife action here, as it's a prime summer nesting beach for loggerhead sea turtles. Nothing on Kiawah is too far from the beach, which has several access points; beach chairs and umbrellas are available for rent. Although this isn't a major surfer hangout, it is possible to rent ocean kayaks, surfboards, and stand-up paddleboards at Boardwalk #5 in **West Beach** and at the **Sanctuary Beach,** but the offshore waters never get crowded with competitive watersports fanatics. Many guests prefer to lounge by the resort's various swimming pools, and while all the golfers are off hitting the links, you may find sections of the beach pleasantly empty—except for the birds, of course.

ⓘ www.kiawahisland.com.

✈ Charleston International Airport (25 miles/40km).

🏨 $$$ **The Sanctuary Hotel** at Kiawah Island Golf Resort (📞 **877/683-1234**; www.kiawahresort.com).

Natural Wonders 91

Fraser Island
Where Sand Is King
Queensland, Australia

LIKE THE WORLD'S BIGGEST SANDBOX, FRASER ISLAND IS AN ECOLOGICAL marvel made of nothing but sand, lying just south of the Great Barrier Reef. Ancient eucalyptus rainforest grows out of dunes up to 240m high (787 ft.), and an uninterrupted surf-foamed Pacific beach runs the length of the island for an incredible 120km (75 miles). Only problem is . . . you can't swim off that beach, between the fierce offshore currents and the circling sharks. But there's an easy way around that—go inland, where Fraser Island offers so many places to swim, it's as if Mother Nature had designed it as a water park.

Set into the sand dunes of Fraser Island are more than 100 little freshwater lakes, ringed with dazzling white sand that's pure silica—whiter sand than the big Pacific beach, in fact. Some, like brilliant blue **Lake McKenzie,** sprang up when water filled hardened hollows in the dunes; others, like emerald-green **Lake Wabby,** were created when shifting dunes dammed up a stream. Shallow, swift-flowing **Eli Creek** is as much fun as a lazy river ride—wade up the creek for a mile or two and then let the current carry you back down.

Of course you should spend some time on 75-Mile Beach—it's actually a highway you can drive along with a four-wheel-drive vehicle (the only cars allowed on this island). A rusted wrecked luxury steamship, the *Maheno,* sits right on the beach, offering a rare chance for nondivers to see a shipwreck up close; just north of the wreck loom gorgeous erosion-sculpted ocher cliffs called the **Cathedrals.** At the northern end of the beach, you can dip into the ocean in the spa-like bubbling waters of the **Champagne Pools** (also called the Aquarium for their tide-pool marine life), shallow pockets of soft sand protected from the waves by a natural rock barrier.

With no towns and few facilities, apart from low-profile ecotourism resorts, Fraser Island is a no-frills destination for folks who love wildlife better than the wild life. It's a place for camping out, birdwatching, and bush-walking, through eucalyptus woods, wildflower carpeted heath, and fringing mangrove wetlands where dugongs and swamp wallabies thrive. And from August through October, Fraser Island is one of Australia's best sites for seeing humpback whales returning to Antarctica with their calves in tow (book whale watch tours, as well as dolphin or manatee-spotting tours, from local resorts). Dingos run wild here, one of the purest populations anywhere—what's more Australian than that?

ⓘ www.frasercoastholidays.info or www.fraserisland.net.

✈ Hervey Bay (35km/22 miles).

🚢 From Hervey Bay, 45 min.

🛏 $ **Base Camp Fraser Island,** Eurong Beach (ⓒ **61/7/4127 9437;** www.basecampfraserisland.com.au). $$$ **Kingfisher Bay Resort,** west coast (ⓒ **61/7/4194 9300;** www.kingfisherbay.com).

Sylt

Shape-Shifting in the North Sea
Germany

BEAUTIFUL PEOPLE FLOCK TO THE ISLAND OF SYLT—ONE OF GERMANY'S most chic and expensive resort spots—to browse the upscale boutiques of Kampen, lounge on the white-sand beaches of Rantum, and "take the cure" at the spas of Wenningstedt, from mud baths to sunshine therapy (a fancy name for nude sunbathing). But there's a distinct fiddling-while-Rome-burns quality to it all. This long, skinny West Frisian island—the northernmost place in Germany—is practically nothing but beach, and that beach is disappearing every day.

In fact, Sylt (pronounced *Zoolt*) has existed only since 1362, when the Great Mandrenke flood deposited so much sediment in the sea that it built up into a long T-shaped sand spit running parallel to the coast of Denmark. The island is still only about 550m (1,800 ft.) wide at its narrowest point, depending on which day you measure it. While Sylt is pummeled by North Sea surf on the west, the tranquil Wadden Sea on the east is so shallow, it turns to marshy mud flats at low tide (attracting hordes of migratory water birds, it has become a bird sanctuary). Reminders of Sylt's exposure lie everywhere—in the iodine tang of the air, the constant whipping winds, the rain-soaked climate that Germans call *Reiz-klima;* even the most fashion-conscious visitors regularly go about in yellow slickers, nicknamed "Sylt mink."

Sylt's sand dunes shift by as much as 3 to 4m (10–13 ft.) a year, despite ongoing efforts to stabilize them by planting marram grass and hardy wild Siberian roses. Sheep are grazed on man-made sea dikes, in hopes they'll pack down the soil with their hooves. But storm surges continue to gnaw away at the land; on some mornings after violent storms, vast areas of beach simply disappear, sucked out into the North Sea. While sunbathing on Sylt's soft white strands, in the distance you'll see barges pumping sand from offshore depths, which will later be dumped by bulldozers back onto the fugitive beaches.

Every year on the night of February 21, the islanders celebrate **Biikebrennen,** an ancient pagan rite in which towering stacks of wood on the beaches are set ablaze, lighting the night sky. Afterward, everyone adjourns to local restaurants for a traditional dinner featuring savory kale (distinctly seaweedy in appearance), while those bonfires flicker on through the long northern night, driving away winter, appeasing the ravenous gods of the sea.

ⓘ http://en.sylt.de.

✈ Sylt.

🛳 From Havneby, Denmark, 40 min. (www.syltfaehre.de).

🛏 $$ **Hotel Wünschmann,** Andreas-Dirks-Strasse 4 (✆ **49/ 4651/5025;** www.hotel-wuenschmann.de). $$$ **Stadt Hamburg,** Strandstrasse 2 (✆ **49/4651/8580;** www.hotelstadthamburg. com).

93 Natural Wonders

Zlatni Rat
Playing the Horn
Brač, Croatia

THE AERIAL VIEW IS BREATHTAKING: A LONG NARROW SPEAR OF golden pebble beach, parting the crystal blue Adriatic waters, with a wedge of dense green pine-oak forest accentuating its V-shape. The Golden Horn is definitely one of Europe's loveliest beaches, yet it's also a freak of nature, its shifting shape completely at the mercy of the wind and sea.

NATURAL WONDERS

Over the past few years, Croatia's affordable, sunny, and drop-dead gorgeous Dalmatian coast has blossomed into one of Europe's hottest travel destinations. And while the party scene tends to focus on trendy Hvar, sporty types are more likely to choose the larger island of Brac, with its temperate Mediterranean climate, rugged unspoiled interior, and great wind and surf. Ferries from the mainland chug into harbor in the main town of **Supetar,** which lies across a channel from Split, Croatia's second largest city and the capital of the Dalmatia region. But thanks to Zlatni Rat, most tourists soon find their way to the southern coast's town of **Bol.** (High-speed catamarans now go directly to Bol from Split.)

Just west of town, the skinny peninsula of Zlatni Rat thrusts .63km (⅓ mile) out into the Adriatic, thickly forested right up to a broad strip of smooth sun-baked pebbles fringing the sea. If you're only used to sand beaches, the pebbles may take a little getting used to—they aren't sharp but they're hard to walk on, and they do get hot. (You can rent beach chairs or umbrellas from kiosks.) Most of Croatia's beaches are pebbled shingles, however, and it doesn't seem to bother the international crew of summertime beachgoers who occupy nearly every inch of that open strand, on both sides of the V. In the afternoons, a stiff westerly mistral wind billows the sails of windsurfers and kiteboarders out on the water, surfers congregate at the Horn's tip, snorkelers explore its stunningly clear waters, and jet-skis zip around the point.

It takes about 20 minutes to walk here from the center of town, although you can also take a water taxi directly to the beach. A backdrop of low rugged mountains makes it feel like more of a wilderness beach than it really is. Busy as it is, Zlatni Rat might have been much more developed and built-up if it weren't a protected natural area, thanks to its unique geomorphology: The beach actually changes its shape and position depending on the wind, currents, and tides. You won't notice it while you sit there, basking in the sun, but sometimes the horn's tip curves to the east, sometimes to the west—it's a curious but subtle phenomenon indeed.

ⓘ www.bol.hr.

✈ Brac.

From Split, 1 hr. ferry to Supetar or 1-hr. catamaran to Bol (www.jadrolinija.hr).

⊨ $$ **Hotel Kaštil,** Frane Radića 1, Bol (© **385/21/63-59-95;** www.kastil.hr). $$$ **Bluesun Hotel Borak,** Bračka Cesta 13, Bol (© **385/21/306-202;** www.brachotelborak.com).

94 Natural Wonders

Mosquito Bay
Glow-in-the Dark Swimming
Vieques, Puerto Rico

IT'S ALMOST LIKE SOMETHING OUT OF A HORROR MOVIE——THE EERIE blue-green glow of the waters around you, responding to every flitting fish and swirling oar. But far from being a ghastly environmental freak, the phosphorescence of Vieques' Mosquito Bay is a one-hundred-percent natural phenomenon, and one you have to see to believe.

Ever since 2003, when the U.S. Navy closed its installation here, the Puerto Rican island of Vieques (pronounced Bee-*ay*-kase) has begun to boom as an eco-friendly—and still charmingly scruffy—destination. With some 40 palm-lined white sand beaches, and reefs of antler coral off shore, for years Vieques has been where Puerto Ricans go to get away from the tourists on the main island, only 7 miles (11km) away. The waterfront of the island's main town, **Isabel Segunda,** is lined with watersports operators, all of whom seem to be related to one another and cheerfully share business.

Among Vieques's many beautiful beaches, perhaps the most popular is **Sombe** (Sun Bay), a mile-long palm-lined stretch of soft coral sand on the south coast just west of Isabel Segunda. East of Sombe, along the same access road, lie two other lovely beaches, the small crescent-shaped **Media Luna** and, down a rutted track, surf-lapped **Navio,** a great place for boogie-boarding and body surfing. Further east yet lies the shallow narrow-mouthed mangrove lagoon of **Mosquito Bay.** In the daytime, it looks like just another lushly overgrown inlet, but return by boat at night and you'll understand why it's nicknamed Phosphorescent Bay: Millions of tiny bioluminescent organisms called pyrodiniums (translation from science-speak: "whirling fire") make its waters glow in the dark. They're only about one-five-hundredths of an inch in size, but when these tiny swimming creatures are disturbed—by, for example, a hovering tour boat—they dart away and light up like fireflies, leaving eerie blue-white trails of phosphorescence. These pyrodiniums exist elsewhere, but not in such amazing concentrations: A gallon of water in Mosquito Bay may contain upward of three-quarters of a million such creatures.

You can even slip off the boat and swim in these glowing waters, a sensation that's incredibly eerie and cool. Don't make the mistake of coming here on a full moon, however—the glow of the pyrodiniums is only discernible on a cloudy, moonless night. (Warning: Some tour boats go out to the bay regardless of the full moon—and you won't get your money back if you're disappointed.) **Island Adventures** (☏ **787/741-0720;** www.biobay.com) operates 2-hour nighttime trips in Phosphorescent Bay aboard the *Luminosa,* though not during the full moon.

✈ Vieques.

🚢 Isabel Segunda (1¼-hr. from Fajardo, P.R).

🛏 $$ **Crow's Nest,** Rte. 201, Barrio Florida (☏ **787/741-0033;** www.crowsnestvieques.com). $$ **Trade Winds Guesthouse,** Calle Flamboyan 107, Esperanza (☏ **787/741-8666;** www.tradewindsvieques.com).

Vieques, Puerto Rico.

Blowing Rocks Preserve
Spouting Off

Jupiter Island, Florida, U.S.A.

UP AT THE NORTH END OF THE MIAMI SPRAWL, NATURE FINALLY GETS room to breathe again. At the south end of Jupiter Island, a barrier island between the Atlantic and Indian River Lagoon, it almost seems as if the ocean is breathing a gasp of relief. At high tide or after winter storms, waves crash against a rubbly shoreline ridge, squeeze through tiny erosion holes, and spout sky-high with a whistling shriek—hence the beach's name, Blowing Rocks.

The Atlantic coast's largest outcropping of Anastasia limestone may look like Hawaiian lava-flow, but it's actually formed of shell, coral, and tiny fossils, compressed into dark jagged ledges. Anastasia limestone—also known as coquina rock—rarely protrudes above ground like this, let alone in such dramatic masses. Winds and waves have carved this unusual outcropping into chimneys and shelves, burrows, rocky pools, and the blow holes that give this beach its name. Even when the waves aren't spouting like geysers, it's an incredibly cool sight. It's hard to believe that this wild scene of nature happens only 25 miles (40km) north of glitzy Palm Beach, but it does—largely because the Nature Conservancy has protected this 73-acre (30 hectare) preserve since 1969.

Enter the preserve through a tunnel of thick evergreen sea grapes and take a 1 mile-long (1.6km) hike along the oceanfront dunes. Coastal hammocks are planted with local sabal palms and the distinctive gumbo-limbo tree (nicknamed the "tourist tree" because its peeling red bark looks like a sunburned tourist). Across the highway, the preserve backs onto the **Indian River Lagoon** estuary, where a boardwalk trail passes mangrove wetlands, tidal flats, and oak hammock (look for fiddler crabs and manatees). It's like a minicourse in Florida habitats; there's even a butterfly garden featuring native plants.

No wonder loggerhead, green, and leatherback sea turtles come back to this beach year after year to lay clutches of eggs from May to August, burying them at night in the warm sand (look for turtle tracks in the sand in the mornings). Nesting areas may be roped off during nesting season; please respect prohibited areas.

During preserve hours (Mon–Fri 9am–4:30pm) you can swim, snorkel, or scuba diving off this protected beach. The rocks and worm-rock reefs offshore offer great opportunities for snorkeling or scuba diving. Best of all, stand atop the dunes and appreciate one of the few Florida beaches that escaped being turned into a white-sand cliche.

ⓘ **Blowing Rocks Preserve,** 574 S. Beach Rd., State Rd. A1A (✆ **561/744-6668**).

✈ Palm Beach.

🛏 $$$ **Jupiter Beach Resort,** 5 N. A1A, Jupiter (✆ **866/943-0950** or 561/746-2511; www.jupiterbeachresort.com). $$ **Jupiter Waterfront Inn,** 18903 SE Federal Highway, Jupiter (✆ **888/747-9085;** www.jupiterwaterfrontinn.com).

96 Natural Wonders

Hot Water Beach
Spa on the Sand
Coromandel Peninsula, New Zealand

ON NEW ZEALAND'S NORTH ISLAND, THERMAL SPRINGS AND POOLS spout and bubble everywhere, most famously at the spa town of Rotorua. By all means visit Rotorua while you're here, but then head north to the rugged Coromandel Peninsula, where thermal pools crop up right on a lovely sandy beach—your own natural beachfront hot tub.

Beach-goers enjoy a soak in self-dug holes at Hot Water Beach.

Hot Water Beach lies just south of the Coromandel's largest town, Whitianga, which means "crossing place" in Maori. The legendary Maori explorer Kupe first settled this area around 950 A.D.; Captain James Cook sailed in 1769 and named its sweeping bay Mercury Bay, after observing the transit of Venus from what is now called Cook's Beach. Whitianga is charmingly laidback, and Mercury Bay is lovely—but the really spectacular stuff is around the headlands, facing the open Pacific. A classic day trip out of Whitianga heads south on Purangi Road to pristine **Hanei Beach** and its adjacent marine reserve, anchored by majestic Cathedral Cove. It's only a few miles further south down Link Road to the tiny hamlet of **Hot Water Beach,** an obvious add-on to this excursion—but you've got to time it right. Arrive no more than 2 hours before or 2 hours after low tide, for that's when the hot waters of an underground river, flowing into the Pacific, seep up into the golden sands.

It's a handsome beach, overlooking the Pacific and offshore **Castle Rock;** cliffs at either end of the beach are densely covered with hardy green pohutukawa trees, also known as the New Zealand Christmas tree because they burst into bright red blooms in December and January (New Zealand's summer). Although the beach is relatively deserted for most of the day, during that 4-hour window a busy crowd of beachgoers show up, bathing suits on, sand shovels in hand. (If you haven't brought one, you can easily pick one up at a shop right by the parking lot.) Dig a hole in the sand and you can settle in, soaking in the warm mineral-rich water that surges into your sandy hollow. Thanks to underground volcanic fissures, this superheated water may be as hot as 147°F (64°C) and flows at a rate of up to 15 liters per minute. It's an irresistibly fun experience—the people on either side of you will be giggling with delight, and you might as well join in.

ⓘ www.whitianga.co.nz.

✈ Whitianga.

🛏 $$ **Admiralty Lodge,** 69-71 Buffalo Beach Rd., Whitianga (ⓒ **64/7/866-0181;** www.admiraltylodge.co.nz). $$ **Beachfront Resort,** 113 Buffalo Beach Rd., Whitianga (ⓒ **64/7/866-5637;** www.beachfrontresort.co.nz).

97   Natural Wonders

Pink Sands Beach
Pretty in Pink
Harbour Island, The Bahamas

IT'S NOT THE ONLY PINK BEACH IN THE CARIBBEAN, BUT IT APPEARS SO often on Most Beautiful Beach lists, it's a safe bet to call Pink Sands Beach the fairest of them all. Running along almost the entire eastern side of small Harbour Island—one of the Bahamas' Out Islands, aka Family Islands—Pink Sands Beach is a 4.8km-long (3-mile) stretch of powdery soft pale pink sand, backed by green palms and lapped by turquoise waters. Forget black-and-white photos—even color shots don't do this place justice.

Beauty is as beauty does, of course, and Pink Sands Beach is also a great swimming beach, its calm waters protected by an off-shore reef. With a climate that ranges between an average 72°F (22°C) in winter and 82°F (28°C) in summer, Pink Sands is good for water sports all year round. A few villas and low-rise hotels stand behind the palm trees, but there are no bars or beach stands to disturb the refined, quiet atmosphere. There's always plenty of room on those blushing sands, which can be anywhere from 1835m (50–100 ft.) wide.

So what makes these sands so pink? There's crushed coral, of course, mixed with ground shells and rock, but the color mostly comes from teensy fragments of the bright-pink shells of micro-scopic insects called Foraminifera, which live in abundance on the underside of that sheltering reefs. Come here at sunrise to watch the sand gradually glow to life as the day begins.

Harbour Island seems today like an outlier in the 700-plus-island Bahamas archipelago, which for most modern visitors centers around heavily developed Grand Bahama, New Providence (Nassau), and Paradise Island. Lying only 3.2km (2 miles) east of Eleuthera, Harbour Island is only reachable by boat—a sort of seclusion that seems to suit the wealthy trendsetters who congregate here, puttering about the tiny island in golf carts and on bicycles. Harbour Island (or as it was originally called, Briland) was the Bahamas' original capital, however, and its main village, **Dunmore Town,** is still full of historic charm, with old pastel-colored gingerbread cottages, white picket fences draped in bougainvillea, and car-free lanes. But make no mistake: Harbour Island is an expensive, exclusive getaway—no wonder those sands are blushing.

ⓘ www.harbourislandguide.com.

✈ Eleutherea, a 3-km (2-mile) motorboat ride from Harbour Island.

From Nassau, 2 hr. (www.bahamasferries.com).

$$$ **Coral Sands,** Chapel St. (✆ **888/568-5493** or 242/333-2350; www.coralsands.com). $$$ **Pink Sands Resort,** Chapel St. (✆ **800/407-4776** or 242/333-2030; www.pinksandsresort.com).

98 Natural Wonders

Spiaggia Sabbie Nere
Vulcan's Hideaway
Vulcano, Italy

THE ENCHANTING MEDITERRANEAN ISLAND OF SICILY IS SO LARGE, IT has its own islands—including a breezy seven-island archipelago off its north coast that the ancient Romans named the Aeolians, after Aeolus, the god of winds. Even more appropriately, they named the chain's southernmost island Vulcano, after the Roman god of fire (eventually all the world's volcanoes would be named after this island). Just look at its dark jagged mountains, smoking craters, and bubbling sulfurous mud—no wonder they believed Vulcan's private forge lay underground. With all that volcanic activity, it's only natural that Vulcano's beaches feature stunning basalt-black sands.

Lying 25km (15 miles) north of Sicily, Vulcano gets plenty of vacationers from May through September. (It's only a 15-min. ferry hop from neighboring Lipari, the Aeolian island with the most hotels.) Given the torrid heat of Sicilian summers, many visitors head straight for the island's best beach: Spiaggia Sabbie Nere. It's only a 20-minute walk from the ferry port, Porto di Levante, east across the island to Porto di Ponente. The sands are black indeed, but fine and soft (most of Vulcano's other beaches are pebbly), and the water is shallow and good for swimming. A few jagged offshore rocks and the backdrop of brooding mountains make this crescent incredibly picturesque. Naturally it gets crowded in summer, but the vibe is sociable. Those black sands retain heat, so you may want to rent a beach chair or umbrella from one of the stabilimenti (beach clubs) lining the beach. The beachfront pizzeria/bar Zammara is perennially popular.

Before or after the beach, take time to explore a little more of this weird and wonderful island. Near the docks, you'll smell the **Laghetti dei Fanghi** before you see it; it's a sludgy pool of naturally radioactive mud that spa-goers believe will cure all sorts of ills. Head for the northern peninsula of Vulcanetto to scramble around a rugged landscape of twisted volcanic rocks, fancifully nicknamed **Valle dei Mostri,** or Valley of Monsters. A vigorous 1-hour hike from Porto di Levante (count on 3 hr. for a round-trip) will take you atop the island's biggest volcano, **Vulcano della Fossa.** Vulcano della Fossa is still active, though it hasn't erupted since 1890; beware the hissing cracks in the lunarlike landscape, where super-heated gases burst out. When you finally reach the rim of its steamy crater, stare down and imagine, as the Greek poet Homer did in the Odyssey, that it's the gateway to Hades. Vulcan himself could be watching.

✈ Palermo/Catania.

🚢 From Milazzo, Sicily, 40–90 min. (**Siremar,** www.siremar.it; or **Ustica Lines,** www.usticalines.it). From Naples, Italy, 4 hr. (www.snav.it).

🛏 $$ **Hotel Conti,** Via Porta Ponente, Vulcano (✆ **39/90/985-2012;** www.contivulcano.it) $$ **Hotel Garden,** Porta Ponente (✆ **39/90/985-2106;** www.hotelgardenvulcano.com).

Natural Wonders

Punalu'u Beach & Papakeola Beach

Sand of a Different Color

The Big Island, Hawaii, U.S.A.

FLYING IN A HELICOPTER OVER HAWAII VOLCANOES NATIONAL PARK IS a jaw-dropping experience. Active volcanoes simmer and seethe beneath you; red-hot lava glows in the caldera, and you can trace paths of lava flow trailing down to the sea. No wonder it's one of the most popular excursions on the Big Island of Hawaii.

Fewer visitors, however, continue west on Highway 11 from the park to see the stunning results of that volcanic activity. Here on the southern tip of Hawaii, a couple miles west of Pahala, turn off the highway onto Punaluu Road to magnificent **Punalu'u Beach.** Hawaii has other black sand beaches, but palm-lined Punalu'u is the most accessible one, and it's covered in true black sand—not just chipped lava carried down river beds, but black basalt pulverized as it meets the cold ocean. Run this black sand through your fingers and you'll see how fine it is. The ocean floor is too rocky for decent swimming (the water's also strangely cold, fed by an underground spring). But hawksbill and green sea turtles love it, basking on the black sands in such numbers, you'll forget that these are actually endangered species. The endangered 'io (Hawaiian hawk) nests in the trees, Hawaiian monk seals loll on offshore rocks, and spinner dolphins and humpback whales often sail so close, you can spot them from shore.

It takes more effort to get to **Papakolea Beach,** which lies further west, past Naalehu near jagged South Point (Ka Lae), the island's utmost tip. Turn off Highway 11 onto South Point Road and follow it south to the end (bear left at the fork). Park your car, then hike 2½ miles (4km) east along the clifftop dirt track to Mahana Bay. (You may see some people driving this rutted road, but that's best left to experienced off-road drivers.) At the end you'll be rewarded with an incredible sight: a long slope of smooth olive-green sand, cupped in the giant bowl of a half-collapsed cinder cone, **Pu'u o Mahana.** It's one of only two green sand beaches in the world (the other is in Guam). Climb down the cliff face to get a closer look: Ocean waves eroding the cone's ridged inner walls deposit upon the sand tiny crystals of olivine, a volcanic byproduct that forms from cooling magma. Large chunks of olivine, polished into a gemstone, are called peridot, or—the local name—Hawaiian Diamond (it's also responsible for the sparkle of the famous Diamond Head on Oahu). After that hike, you may be tempted to swim, but beware of turbulent waters. There's a lot of ocean between here and the next continental landfall: Antarctica.

ⓘ www.bigisland.org.

✈ Hilo or Kona.

🛏 $$ **Kilauea Lodge,** 19-3948 Old Volcano Rd., Volcano Village (© **808/967-7366;** www.kilauealodge.com). $ **Uncle Billy's Kona Bay,** 75-5739 Alii Dr., Kona (© **800/367-5102** or 808/961-5818; www.unclebilly.com).

The green sand beach Pu'u o Mahana.

Sleeping Bear Dunes National Lakeshore

The Mega-Dunes of Michigan

Empire, Michigan, U.S.A.

OCEAN BEACHES USUALLY GRAB ALL THE AWARDS, BUT WHAT ABOUT lake shores? The Great Lakes are made of fresh water, not saltwater, but they're so huge they might as well be seas. Standing on the eastern shore of Lake Michigan, you can gaze west at water as far as the eye can see, your feet deep in glorious white sand. In August 2011, a viewer poll conducted by the TV show *Good Morning America* named Michigan's Sleeping Bear Dunes as the Most Beautiful Place in America. Encompassing 65 miles (104km) of Lower Michigan's lakefront—plus inland lakes and two big islands—Sleeping Bear Dunes National Lakeshore offers not just one beach, but a number of soft white-sand beaches to explore.

Naturally you'll want to hike around the namesake dunes themselves, which rise an impressive 450 ft (122m) above the lapping lake waters below. North of the town of Empire, **Sleeping Bear Plateau** is an immense dune field about 5 miles long (8km) and 3 miles wide (5km), composed of "perched" dunes, sitting on top of already-tall coastal bluffs formed of glacial moraines. As waves erode the faces of those moraines, winds swoop up loosened sand and gravel and heap it atop the bluffs, in great mounds that really do resemble sleeping bears. Three hiking trails off of Highway 109 let you scramble around these big soft mountains of sand. Doing the **Dune Climb** is a classic ritual of Michigan childhood; once you've made it to the top, you can slip and slide back down the soft white slopes to the picnic area, or else hike on over the dunes to the lake, a strenuous 3½ miles (5.6km) round-trip.

Elsewhere along the lakeshore, undulating shoreline dunes back sandy beaches which are enormously popular in summer, despite how chilly Lake Michigan can be in June (it warms up in July and Aug). Two of the most popular swimming beaches are **Peterson Beach,** at the end of gravelly Peterson Road, and **North Bar Lake,** where a line of dunes separates a warm shallow lake from the more bracing waves of Lake Michigan. At the end of M-22, just south of Empire, quiet **Esch Beach** lies at the mouth of Otter Creek, where you can wade in the shallows; tubing and kayaking trips along the Platte River end up on the soft sands of **Platte Point Beach.** And humans aren't the only beach lovers here—the last of the Great Lakes' piping plovers nest on the beaches from late April through August, so be sure to respect roped-off nesting areas.

ⓘ www.nps.gov/slbe.

✈ Traverse City (24 miles/39km).

🛏 $$ **The Homestead,** 1 Wood Ridge Rd., Glen Arbor (ⓒ 231/334-5000; www.thehomesteadresort.com). $$ **Glen Arbor Lakeshore Inn,** 5793 S. Ray St., Glen Arbor (ⓒ **231/334-3773;** www.lakeshoreinnmotel.com).

Geographical Index

Photo Credits

NOTES